547-6166

OSPREY
PUBLISHING

British Infantryman in the Far East 1 5

Alan Jeffreys • Illustrated by Kevin Lyles & Jeff Vanelle

First published in Great Britain in 2003 by Osprey Publishing,
Elms Court, Chapel Way, Botley, Oxford OX2 9LP, United Kingdom.
Email: info@ospreypublishing.com

A CIP catalogue record for this book is available from the British Library.

ISBN 1 84176 448 5

Editor: Tom Lowres
Design: Ken Vail Graphic Design, Cambridge, UK
Index: Alan Rutter
Originated by Grasmere Digital Imaging, Leeds, UK
Printed in China through World Print Ltd.

03 04 05 06 07   10 9 8 7 6 5 4 3 2 1

For a catalogue of all books published by Osprey Military and Aviation please
contact:

Osprey Direct UK, P.O. Box 140, Wellingborough, Northants, NN8 2FA, UK
E-mail: info@ospreydirect.co.uk

Osprey Direct USA, c/o MBI Publishing, P.O. Box 1, 729 Prospect Ave,
Osceola, WI 54020, USA
E-mail: info@ospreydirectusa.com

www.ospreypublishing.com

Artist's note

Readers may care to note that the original paintings from
which the colour plates in this book were prepared are
available for private sale. All reproduction copyright
whatsoever is retained by the Publishers. All enquiries
should be addressed to:

Kevin Lyles,
Hill View,
38 Boswick Lane,
Dudswell,
Berkhamsted,
HP4 3TE,
UK

The Publishers regret that they can enter into no
correspondence upon this matter.

Editor's note

All the photographs are courtesy of the Trustees of the
Imperial War Museum and can be ordered from the
Photograph Archive.

Acknowledgements

Thanks to Mike Hibberd, Simon Robbins, Paul Cornish and
all my colleagues in the Department of Exhibits and
Firearms. Thanks also to my battlefield touring companions
Gerard Chappell and Toby Padgham and I am very grateful
to Mike Taylor for all his assistance.

Author's dedication

For Lorraine and Michael.

CONTENTS

BRITISH INFANTRYMAN IN THE FAR EAST 1941–45

INTRODUCTION

In just five months, from December 1941 to May 1942, the British Empire suffered the most humiliating series of defeats in its history as Hong Kong, Malaya, Borneo, Singapore and Burma fell in rapid succession to the seemingly unstoppable Imperial Japanese Army. The fall of Singapore in February 1942 was the biggest defeat suffered by British and Commonwealth forces during World War II, when 130,000 armed forces personnel surrendered to the Japanese, while the retreat from Burma was the longest retreat in British military history. Two years later, the 14th Army, after thorough training, was able to defeat the Japanese

General Slim, commander of 14th Army, examining a Japanese flag presented to him by the 7th Gurkha Rifles captured at Imphal. Note the 14th Army formation sign which was designed by Slim himself. Red and black represented the colours of the British and Indian armies and the sword pointed downwards, against heraldic convention, because he knew that the 14th Army would have to reconquer Burma from the north. The hilt formed an S for Slim and on the handle was the army's title in morse code. (courtesy of the Trustees of the Imperial War Museum)

forces at the battles of Kohima and Imphal and then went on to retake Burma, in its turn inflicting the biggest land defeat on the Japanese Army. This transformation in the fortunes of the British soldier was largely due to the development and improvement in tactics, training and equipment.

These campaigns were largely fought in the jungle, which was a terrifyingly alien environment on first acquaintance for nearly all the British troops. The word 'jungle' is Indian in origin and means wasteland but it has been used to describe anything from sparsely wooded areas to tropical forest. Until the World War II the jungle was usually described as bush or forest in military circles. Generally there were two types of jungle, (1) primary jungle, usually defined as natural jungle growth with poor visibility and little undergrowth, and (2) secondary jungle, which was cleared primary jungle that had regrown and consisted of very dense undergrowth, severely limiting movement. The jungle was beset with the problems of difficult climate, terrain, vegetation, wildlife and tropical disease such as malaria. Added to these were the tactical limitations imposed by the jungle; with its limited observation and fields of fire, communication problems, lack of mobility and long lines of supply. These problems all needed to be overcome to produce troops capable of defeating the Japanese. As a War Office publication stated in 1945:

Two soldiers of the 1st Battalion, Queen's Royal Regiment, at the Sittang Bend where the Queen's Royal Regiment undertook its last action in Burma. (courtesy of the Trustees of the Imperial War Museum)

It may be difficult for anyone without experience of jungle warfare to realize how close were the distances at which most of the battles were fought. A grenade might be lobbed or rolled a few yards; a burst would be fired from the hip; a Japanese officer's sword would be struck from his grasp by a rifle and bayonet. In this type of fighting there was no substitute for infantry, and there was a danger that the fullest use might not be made of tanks, artillery, and all other supporting arms. This danger had to be watched constantly, and plans so framed that the infantry should have the weightiest support that ground and weather allowed our tremendous superiority in supporting fire to give them.

Thus the infantryman was of paramount importance for fighting in the jungles of South-East Asia.

This book will consider the experience of the British infantryman who fought in the Far East, ranging from Malaya to Burma and India. It will cover conventional jungle warfare rather than special forces such as the Chindits, V Force and Force 136. The majority of the forces fighting in this theatre were Indian Army. An Indian Army division was composed of three brigades, each of three battalions, of which one would be a British Army battalion. In addition, there were two British Army divisions in theatre, two West African divisions and 11th East African Division, all commanded and led by British officers and non-commissioned officers (NCOs). This book will also look at the training and combat experience of the British troops fighting in Malaya and Burma, in particular the 2nd Battalion, Argyll and Sutherland Highlanders, in 12th Indian Infantry Brigade in Malaya, and the 1st Battalion, Queen's Royal Regiment (West Surrey), of 7th Indian Division, Burma, of 14th Army, which consisted of 4, 15 and 23 Indian Corps and was disbanded in December 1945.

2nd Battalion, Argyll and Sutherland Highland Regiment, on the march. (courtesy of the Trustees of the Imperial War Museum)

CHRONOLOGY

1939

28 September   2nd Battalion, Argyll and Sutherland Highlanders, arrive in Singapore to form part of 12th Indian Infantry Brigade

1941

19 February   8th Australian Division land in Singapore

2 December   Force Z consisting of HMS *Prince of Wales*, HMS *Repulse* and 4 destroyers arrive in Singapore

7 December   Japanese forces invade Malaya and attack Pearl Harbor

10 December   HMS *Repulse* and HMS *Prince of Wales* sunk off the eastern coast of Malaya

18–19 December Japanese invade Hong Kong

25 December   Surrender of Hong Kong

1942

7 January   Japanese forces smash through the 12th and 28th Indian Infantry Brigades at the Battle of Slim River

10 January   ABDA (American British Dutch Australian) command set up under General Wavell

11 January   Japanese Army enters Kuala Lumpur

16 January   Japanese forces invade Burma

30 January   British and Commonwealth forces withdraw to Singapore Island; the Argylls bring up the rear playing the bagpipes while crossing the causeway

31 January   Japanese capture Moulmein in Burma

7 February   General Percival, General Officer Commanding (GOC) Malaya, declares that Singapore would be held to the last man after the Japanese land on the island

15 February   Surrender of Singapore

21 February   British and Commonwealth troops withdraw to Sittang Bridge

27 February   Battle of Java Sea

5 March   General Alexander appointed GOC Burma

8 March   Japanese forces enter Rangoon

19 March   General Slim appointed Corps Commander in Burma

29 April   Japanese occupy Lashio and cut the Burma Road

1 May   British evacuate Mandalay

15 May   British and Commonwealth forces retreat across the Burma–India border

4–7 June   Battle of Midway

7–8 August   American forces land on Guadalcanal

5 September   Australian forces defeat the Japanese at Milne Bay in New Guinea

21 September   First Arakan campaign begins

1943

14 February   First Chindit expedition begins

17 March   Japanese counterattack on Arakan Front

12 May   End of disastrous First Arakan campaign

18 June   Wavell becomes Viceroy of India; replaced by General Auchinleck as Commander-in-Chief India

25 August	Lord Louis Mountbatten appointed Supreme Allied Commander in South-East Asia
7 October	Mountbatten arrives in India
21 October	Subhas Chandra Bose forms the 'Government of Free India' in Singapore

1944

9 January	Second Arakan campaign begins
5 February	Second Chindit operation begins
6–25 February	Battle of Admin Box
16 March	Japanese offensive on Imphal Plain begins
24 March	General Orde Wingate killed in plane crash
29 March	Siege of Imphal begins
4 April	Japanese attack Kohima
20 April	Kohima relieved
16 May	Last enemy troops cleared from Kohima Ridge
22 May	Imphal Plain relieved
3 June	End of the battle of Kohima
22 June	Kohima–Imphal road is cleared
10 July	Japanese cleared from the Ukrul area
28 September	Third Arakan campaign begins
2 December	14th Army takes Kalewa

1945

10 January	14th Army takes Shwebo
22 January	Burma Road reopened
19 February	US Marines land on Iwo Jima
22 April	14th Army takes Yenangyaung
4 March	Battle of Meiktila
21 March	Recapture of Mandalay
28 April	Arakan retaken
3 May	Rangoon recaptured by 17th Indian Division
10 May	14th Army links up with troops from the Arakan cutting off Japanese troops west of the Irrawaddy
28 May	14th Army withdraws to India and British 12th Army establish Headquarters (HQ) at Rangoon
6–9 August	Atomic bombs dropped on Hiroshima and Nagasaki
2 September	General MacArthur accepts the surrender of the Japanese at Tokyo Bay on board USS *Missouri* flanked by Generals Percival and Wainwright who had been prisoners of war of the Japanese
12 September	Mountbatten accepts surrender of Japanese forces at Singapore
13 September	Japanese sign surrender for Burma

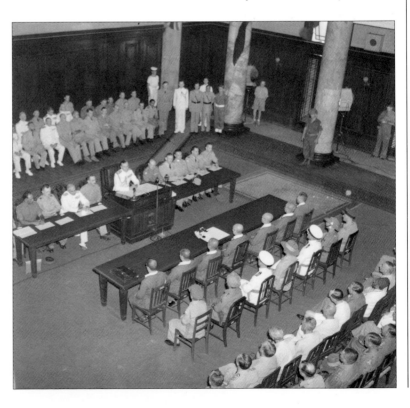

The surrender ceremony in Singapore with the Supreme Allied Commander SEAC, Lord Mountbatten, presiding. (courtesy of the Trustees of the Imperial War Museum)

RECRUITMENT

Conscription was introduced in the Military Training Act of May 1939, but it only applied to men aged 20 and 21 who had to undertake six months' military training and was introduced in order to create five extra Territorial Army divisions of Anti-Aircraft Command. However, on 3 September 1939 the National Service (Armed Forces) Act was passed which meant that all men between 18 and 41 were eligible for 'call-up'. The younger single men were called up first. They had to give their occupation, choose which service they preferred and then had to undertake a medical examination. Registrants were placed into four grades with generally those in the first and second categories taken for active service.

The process of joining up could be hastened through volunteering and during the war 1.5 million volunteered for active service. Men volunteered for various reasons including peer pressure, a sense of adventure, relief from a boring job or in order to acquire a coveted service job. Patriotism was not the factor in recruitment that it was during the World War I. In fact the generation of 1939 was healthier, better educated and had higher expectations than their fathers in 1914. By December 1939 there were 1,128,000 men in the army, and this was divided up into eight geographical commands and districts of both regular and territorial divisions.

An infantry recruit would start his training at a Primary Training Centre (PTCs) and would undergo six weeks' basic infantry training. He would be given injections for typhoid and typhus and would then embark on basic training in drill, shooting, physical training, map reading and tactics. Ultimately, the personnel selection board would decide which arm of service the recruit was best suited for. Officer training was undertaken in officer cadet training units (OCTUs) and varied in length according to the particular arm of service. The course lasted 17 weeks and then the newly trained officers received their commissions before being posted to their regiments. Those who did not make it to officer grade were embarrassingly returned to their unit and nicknamed 'RTUs'.

Prior to the outbreak of war, infantry training took four months in the infantry regimental depot. After 1939, infantry recruits did the six-week basic training and were then sent to Infantry Training Centres (ITCs). This system continued throughout the war and by 1944 nearly 200,000 recruits had undergone basic and infantry training. Officers received training at the Small Arms School at Hythe until the School of Infantry was formed in 1942 at Barnard Castle before moving to Warminster in 1945. The School of Infantry taught three courses for platoon and company commanders as well as commanding officers' courses. The platoon commanders' course was very intensive. The officers took on the roles of men in an infantry platoon. On the first day, training consisted of wading through a river, followed by a cross-country march, ending with a bayonet charge. The officers would be weighed down by the end of the day due to their mud-encased boots and wet clothing. But this was followed by two more 'wet' days when officers would frequently be up to their waists in water. The course culminated in an endurance test in which the infantry platoon was caught by enemy fire and had to lie in often frozen mud while awaiting the cover of a smoke screen to enable them to mount a successful attack against the enemy. In February 1943 the NCOs'

Classification Centre was set up at Bodmin. It became the Infantry NCOs School at Gravesend, moving to High Leigh and then joining with the Infantry School at Warminster. By 1945, 4,500 officers and 10,000 warrant officers (WOs) and NCOs had been trained in the School of Infantry.

Battalions were made up of soldiers, NCOs and officers from other units, as well as new recruits. Battalion training included weapons training, route marching, tactical exercises and specialist training with mortars, Bren carriers, Bren guns and signals. The battalion would live in tents or billets near the regimental depot, and, through training and living together, and regimental history, a battalion *esprit de corps* was instilled into the men. Then brigade and divisional exercises and specialist training such as combined operations would be embarked on.

Often troops did not know their overseas destinations until they were issued tropical kit, and still they could not be certain where they were headed – it could mean North Africa or it might be the Far East. For instance, the units that made up British 2nd Division congregrated in Gloucestershire and Oxfordshire before embarking on the transport ships from Liverpool but little training for the tropics occurred until the unit was actually in theatre.

ARRIVAL IN THE TROPICS

Most soldiers arrived in India after a three-month voyage from Great Britain but none of the lectures aboard ship prepared the troops for India. On arrival in Bombay the troops only had time to notice the smell and heat of the city and then were despatched into trains to take them to their training camps. The train system was the main transit system of India and the trains were much larger than in the UK. The BORs (British 'other ranks') were accommodated in open carriages with wooden benches, with the officers in compartments, while civilians often travelled on the outside of the trains which intrigued those new to India. The trains brought the British Tommies into contact for the first time with *char-wallahs* selling their wares of tea and 'egg banjos' (rolls) costing four *annas*.

Life in the cantonments took time to get used to. The British soldiers found the heat very oppressive and it usually took a couple of months for troops to adapt. The infamous Deolali transit camp was nicknamed 'Doolally Tap', which was slang for going crazy, *tap* being Urdu for fever.

The typical weekday routine started with reveille at 6.00 am with a first parade at 6.45 am and breakfast at 7.30 am. Morning parades from 9.30 am until 1.00 pm and there was a siesta until tea at 4.00 pm and parades again until supper at 7.00 pm. However, in contrast to pre-war military life, the siesta was dropped after the first few weeks and troops began marching and training in the heat of the day rather than resting. Prickly heat affected most new arrivals and could be excruciating, with scratching leading to bleeding and then frequently to infection. Disease was another problem associated with acclimatisation, dysentery being particularly prevalent among unprepared soldiers.

In barracks each man had a *charpoy* which was an Indian-made bed and all kit had to be hung up to prevent it being overrun by ants. Soldiers could also hire Indian servants or bearers to make their beds and do their

The Viceroy of India, Field-Marshal Lord Wavell, having a conversation with Kamal Ram and Naik Nand Singh after they had been presented with their Victoria Crosses. Kamal Ram of the 8th Punjab Regiment was awarded his for service in Italy. Naik Nand Singh of the 1/11th Sikh Regimentreceived the first Victoria Cross awarded to the 7th Indian Division. He led a section up India Hill on the Maungdaw–Buthidaung road where they came under heavy machine-gun fire. He went on single-handedly to capture three trenches that enabled the rest of his platoon to move forward and capture the enemy position. (courtesy of the Trustees of the Imperial War Museum)

washing, which would previously have been unknown to the majority of wartime soldiers. While in the camps, troops undertook the usual chores such as cookhouse fatigues and peeling potatoes in addition to training, but food in the barracks was usually cooked by Indian cooks, *bobajis*, under army supervision. Soldiers would queue up for their food from the kitchens and then run to the soldiers' dining-room to prevent the kite hawks from snaffling their meal en route. Breakfast usually consisted of tinned bacon or sometimes soya-link sausages as an alternative – but were universally hated by British troops – and eggs of the smaller Indian variety with bread and butter. Lunch or 'tiffin' was invariably 'meat and two veg' even in the Indian midday heat. The meat was usually tough slices of water buffalo with potatoes and cabbage as the main vegetables, followed by such favourites as rice pudding or jam roly-poly. The evening meal would be similar to lunch. Physical training was also encouraged and the BORs played football and learnt to swim. The evenings were often spent at the camp cinema or in the canteen enjoying egg and chips.

The introduction of the SEAC (South East Asia Command) newspaper by Mountbatten under the

Vera Lynn, after her tour of the 14th Army, sang to 2,000 British Servicemen at Karachi. She, like everyone else in India, suffered from bedbugs, prickly heat and stomach upsets but was giving up to three performances a day. She travelled into Burma performing in Chittagong and made her way into the Arakan. The ENSA unit consisted of a driver, an officer, an NCO and Len Edwards, Miss Lynn's accompanist, and Vera Lynn, with the piano and technical equipment. Here she is seen in the company of a sergeant wearing the brass shoulder titles of the King's Regiment and the shoulder insignia of the Sind District, India, consisting of a native craft in full sail in white on a maroon square. (courtesy of the Trustees of the Imperial War Museum)

editorship of Frank Owen helped to keep the troops up to date with events not only in their own theatre but in the war generally. There were also ENSA (Entertainments National Service Association) concert parties by 1944 and WAS(B) (Women's Auxiliary Service [Burma]) mobile canteens helped to improve the soldiers' lives. These measures all helped to maintain morale in the Far East but as a War Office publication on morale states:

> Generally, however, it must be said that the morale of overseas forces, except when they were actually engaged in operations, was a continual source of anxiety to the authorities, and that no time was more anxious, especially in India and the Far East, than the period immediately succeeding the defeat of Germany.

A WAS(B) Mobile Canteen No. 3 on the Burma Front in 1944. (courtesy of the Trustees of the Imperial War Museum)

British troops in India, particularly if they were involved in internal security duties suppressing Indian nationalists, could easily become disillusioned. In addition troops in the Far East felt that their efforts were given little publicity and that their amenities were inferior to those enjoyed in other theatres. They were bored, considered themselves forgotten and these complaints even reached parliament. The experience of the poverty and social divisions prevalent in the British Empire in India and Malaya also came as a shock to many of the wartime soldiers. They were unable to comprehend the hierarchical nature of institutions such as the Indian Civil Service or a society where soldiers, officers and men could be shunned socially by those, even in the European community, whom they were there to protect. It has been suggested that these experiences prompted many to vote for the Labour party in the 1945 general election.

Leave usually meant short periods of time in a so-called 'holiday camp' in an Indian Army garrison facility such as at Bangalore, with trips to the cinema and buy the opportunity to buy souvenirs. Until late 1944 there was no home leave at all for British troops. The Python scheme was introduced initially to provide home leave for troops with six years' overseas service, but this period was reduced as improved shipping and manpower resources permitted. By summer 1945 troops were being sent home after three years and four months' service in India and South-East Asia. There was also a 28-day in theatre leave scheme for troops who had served in particularly arduous conditions but did not qualify for home leave under the Python scheme.

Other off-duty pursuits such as visiting brothels were only available in the cities. In Delhi there was an army-run brothel near Hakman's Astoria, nicknamed 'the regimental brothel'. The entrance resembled a cinema where a soldier gave the last three digits of his army number and 5 rupees to the corporal in the booth in return for a chit with a room number on it. The soldier was escorted to the room and given condoms. The girls received weekly medical inspections by the Royal Army Medical Corps. Once this arrangement became known in Britain these 'official' brothels were shut down and Delhi was made out of bounds for BORs not on duty. As a result, the prostitutes went on the streets and the incidence of venereal disease shot up.

Two soldiers browsing in the library of the British Welfare Centre. During 1945 some 650,000 books had been despatched for the army and RAF serving in SEAC. Books were distributed free of charge on a scale of six books per man per year. (courtesy of the Trustees of the Imperial War Museum)

In 1942 there were just three army welfare officers in the whole of India burt measures were taken to rectify the situation. In July 1942 the Amenities, Comforts and Entertainment for the Services (ACES) was set up and a Directorate of Welfare and Education was formed in August 1942. The broadcasting of light entertainment began in July 1943 with two hours every week which was gradually increased. It was hoped to transport all letters to the Far East by air by early 1945. Troops received one 'Air letter card' and one 'Airgraph' with free postage per man per week. Additional air mail could also be sent but the postage had to be paid. Airgraphs had space for about 15 lines of writing. They were then microfilmed centrally and the microfilms were sent to the UK by air and then put in envelopes on arrival. The leave centres were to be improved and there were plans to provide a more varied diet. Production of Indian beer was expanded as was the production of more palatable cigarettes for the troops as opposed to the hated Victory V brand.

By September 1944 welfare in India and the Far East had dramatically improved. For instance, the beer allowance had increased from three to five bottles a month and beer was now imported free of duty. Fifty cigarettes were issued weekly to troops in India, whereas previously none had been issued, and following the establishment of SEAC, the issue had increased from 50 to 100. The V cigarettes were gradually being replaced by a new type containing a larger proportion of American tobacco. Small amenities parcels were distributed during operations from 1944 onwards, including such items as soap, books, writing paper, cigarettes, lighters, handkerchiefs, towels etc., supplied by the Army Comforts Depot in Reading. Thus the general welfare of the troops improved in the last two years of the war but as a low priority it was always competing for transport, and the scarcity of welfare workers remained a problem.

Lieutenant Jim Allen briefing a patrol of D Company of the 2nd Battalion, Green Howards. (courtesy of the Trustees of the Imperial War Museum)

BELIEF AND BELONGING

Morale was important both in India and on the front line. General Slim stressed this in his memoir of the campaign in Burma. He noted that the foundations of morale were spiritual, intellectual and material. The spiritual foundation was the belief that the 14th Army as a whole, whether the troops were Indian, African or British, were fighting a worthy cause, not merely to defend India and reoccupy Burma, but to defeat the Japanese Army as an 'evil force'. The soldiers were now to be kept up to date through conferences so that they all felt part of a team fighting for the same objective and could see that their own individual parts in this objective were important. This included pep talks by senior commanders such as Slim and the Supreme Commander, Lord Mountbatten, which were popularly received. One of Mountbatten's talks to members of the 'forgotten' 14th Army was captured on film, and he commented that the 14th Army was not forgotten – no one had even heard of them!

Lord Louis Mountbatten addressing British officers and men near the Arakan Front. (courtesy of the Trustees of the Imperial War Museum)

The intellectual foundation for increasing morale included the belief that they were capable of defeating the Japanese. This could be shown by example, with the defeat of the Japanese by the Australians at Milne Bay in New Guinea in September 1942. Morale could also be enhanced through training, aggressive patrolling in the jungle and then introducing the troops gradually to the rigours of fighting in the jungle to prove to the soldiers that they could fight in such terrain and defeat the Japanese. The idea of the Japanese 'superman' in the jungle needed to be dispelled and defeating him was the best way to achieve this, particularly as the Japanese soldier was willing to die rather than surrender. This would all increase the confidence of troops, demoralised after defeats in Malaya, Burma and during he First Arakan campaign. The Japanese forces strengthened the Allied soldiers' resolve by their treatment of prisoners of war and by committing atrocities in battle, such as the bayoneting and killing of patients and medical personnel at the Main Dressing Station during the battle of the Admin Box, which enraged the defending Commonwealth soldiers and increased their loathing of the enemy. The material foundations for morale included increasing efficiency, improved rest and reinforcement camps, setting up training divisions, improving discipline and the separation of SEAC from India Command.

In addition to these foundations, a loyalty to the 14th Army and the individual British, Indian and African divisions was fostered through the use of formation signs and training and by the men going into action together. However, in the Far East as elsewhere, the fundamental loyalty of the soldier was to his immediate peer group and typically to his own

British and Gurkha troops on the march. They held a great respect for each others fighting abilities. (courtesy of the Trustees of the Imperial War Museum)

infantry section. Each battalion normally had four rifle companies as well as a 3in. mortar companies. Each company, in turn, was split into three platoons and each platoon into three sections of about ten men or less, but usually more than six. Even within the section a soldier usually had a 'mucker' or mate with whom he 'brewed up', the pair looking after each other in and out of action. This was the usual foundation for comradeship among infantrymen and it kept individuals going through the tremendous hardships of fighting the Japanese and the jungle.

TRAINING

In *Notes from Theatres of War No. 19: Burma, 1943/44* we see:

It was the experience of 14th Army that a formation that had trained in the jungle, though it lacked battle experience, was initially better fitted for operations in the jungle than one that had previously been in battle but not in the jungle. The ideal was for a formation to complete its individual and collective training – with particular emphasis on individual training – in normal country, and then spend three months in the jungle, before it was launched into active operations.

Malaya was a relatively quiet garrison posting for British soldiers until the Japanese invasion. The climate was very hot and humid all year round and regiments usually packed up at noon in order to avoid the hottest part of the day. Little training of any kind occurred, few of the formations in Malaya carried out any specific jungle training, and levels of activity depended on the initiative of the individual commanders rather than Malaya Command.

For many years the jungle was classed as impenetrable for troops, hence the lack of interest in jungle training, but a number of surveys and exercises had been undertaken during the 1930s to test this assumption. For example, Brigadier F. H. Vinden, who took the post of General Staff Officer Grade 2 (GSO II) in Malaya Command in 1937, challenged the idea that an invasion in the north of Malaya during the monsoon season was impossible. He sailed up the coast and found Chinese junks landing on the east coast in order to avoid Malaya's immigration quotas. He also destroyed the myth of the impenetrable jungle after an exercise with three British battalions and the Johore Defence Force against an attacking battalion of Gordon Highlanders. The Gordons' commanding officer had had jungle experience in West Africa and Vinden told how 'he sent his attack through the jungle, considered impenetrable, and caught the defence in the rear. Another Malayan myth was destroyed.' To counteract this threat Vinden suggested an increase in the number of troops who 'would have to be trained in jungle warfare about which, even me, knew little'.

By 1940 there were two training manuals available for fighting in Malaya: *Tactical Notes for Malaya*, produced by Malaya Command, and Military Training Pamphlet (MTP) No. 9 (India), *Notes on Forest Warfare*, produced in India. However, due to the need for building defences, the policy of 'milking' units of experienced personnel for the expansion of the Indian Army, and the lack of a central directive for training from Malaya Command, most units did not use these as a basis for training.

Argylls having a rest on the march back from training in Mersing. (courtesy of the Trustees of the Imperial War Museum)

The most notable exception was the 2nd Battalion, Argyll and Sutherland Highlanders, the British battalion in 12th Indian Infantry Brigade. In 1940 the battalion was commanded by Lieutenant-Colonel Ian Stewart, who took a keen interest in training to fight in the jungle, particularly as the brigade was to act as the mobile reserve in the event of an invasion. Stewart thought it took six months for a unit to get fully acclimatised to the jungle. He realised that control of the roads was vital and this would be best maintained through thorough mobility in the jungle rather than through static defence. He developed tactics for the jungle that included 'filleting', which was an encircling attack to the rear of the enemy combined with a frontal attack that would split the opposing force. Special patrols called 'tiger patrols' were introduced, so called as they were meant to trouble the enemy like tigers. These consisted of three to five men going behind enemy lines, not just for reconnaissance but to attack the enemy and break his morale. Stewart had also recognised the importance of good sustenance in the jungle. Realising that the field service ration was unsuitable he built up reserves of alternative provisions for his troops, allowing in particular the issue of hot sweet tea five times a day in the field. He made sure that all troops in the battalion were trained in jungle warfare and even the pioneer and anti-aircraft platoons became experts, although by the Japanese invasion only a third of the battalion was sufficiently trained because of the continual 'milking' of the battalion, including the transfer of 30 Argylls to orderly duties at Malaya Command. Because of Stewart's training drive the battalion was nicknamed 'the jungle beasts'.

In contrast to the situation in Malaya the problem of fighting in the Burmese jungle had to an extent been previously studied and practised, albeit by paramilitary units such as the Burma Frontier Force, which consisted of recruits from Burmese tribes such as the Karens and the Chins under British and Indian Army officers. These forces had seen intermittent irregular jungle warfare operations against tribesmen since the nineteenth century, but were unsuited to and untrained for action against a well-armed and trained conventional enemy. In the event these units were nevertheless used as conventional forces rather than for reconnaissance, the role for which they were trained and equipped. Of the conventional forces in Burma, the 2nd Battalion of the Gloucestershire Regiment had been in the country since 1938. Under their new commander, Lieutenant-Colonel Charles Bagot, they had improved their overall fitness and stamina through a programme of long day and night marches. They had also managed to do some jungle fighting, in fortnightly periods, although the jungle in Burma had been placed out of bounds to troops as a medical hazard.

Following the loss of Malaya and Burma in 1942 the army in India made immediate attempts to learn from the experience of these campaigns. Lessons were learnt from the numerous reports written and individuals such as Stewart and some of his Argylls were evacuated from Singapore to help with training for jungle warfare. In the various training schools and establishments around India they gave lectures about Japanese tactics and the lessons that could be taken from the defeat and Stewart gave a radio broadcast. Major Richard Storry, another evacuee from Singapore, heard a lecture by Stewart at the Intelligence School at Karachi:

> The Lecture was a most outspoken, in parts bitter indictment of the higher planning & conduct of operations in Malaya. Mistakes of strategy & tactics were analysed, Jap methods described and Col Stewart's own theories of counteracting them explained. It was a merciless post-mortem which impressed us all. This lecture Stewart gave, I heard, up & down India that Spring 1942. Later he was one of those who directed the training of units for operations in Burma; so much, I think, is owed to him.

After the lecture tours in India, the evacuated Argylls made up No. 6 GHQ Training Team who organised training exercises and lectures for 14th Indian Division and 2nd Division.

Reorganisation within the divisional structure was instigated in 1942 to overcome some of the problems arising from over-reliance on roads in the recent campaigns. Mechanisation was reduced in the 7th, 20th and 23rd Indian Divisions, and the 17th and 39th Indian Divisions were converted to light divisions, with six-mule companies and four-jeep companies each, in order to operate away from the road. Other administrative changes included the establishment of Central Command to relieve the army commanders of other areas with internal security problems only, and to take on some of the responsibility for administration and training.

The 14th Indian Division underwent intensive jungle training and set up a jungle warfare school at Comilla, Arakan, for the division. The

British troops training in full equipment. (courtesy of the Trustees of the Imperial War Museum)

syllabus covered six key areas: the use of the 'hook' and outflanking movements; maintaining ground having been outflanked in order to keep the initiative; good minor tactics such as ambushing; dispelling the myth of the impenetrable jungle; health discipline; and fitness. There was also training in co-operation with a field artillery regiment. But once again the details of training were mainly down to individual divisional commanders and there was no central directive from GHQ India. Indeed one officer commented that jungle training was still in its infancy and 'bungle warfare' was a better description of the efforts to date. The other factors that delayed training included the Cripps Mission, and the resultant 'Quit India' movement in the summer of 1942 that led to civil unrest, mainly in Eastern Army's area. It took 57 infantry battalions to deal with internal security. This had knock-on effects for airfield construction, factory production of arms, clothing and equipment. In addition, the monsoon of 1942 was very heavy and was followed by a terrible malaria epidemic. There were also uprisings in the Sind and North-West Frontier provinces.

The lack of a central doctrine and direction from GHQ India, together with the poor standard of reinforcements, were instrumental in the defeat of the First Arakan campaign in 1942–43 and in the subsequent poor overall morale in the Army in India. The position was exacerbated because some units had been in continuous action for five months. As a consequence an Infantry Committee was convened to examine ways to remedy the problems and sat for the first two weeks of June 1943. The defeats in Malaya and Burma were blamed on 'milking' to feed the expansion of the Indian Army, failure to recognise the importance of infantry; the lack of basic training and of experienced leadership; fighting on two fronts; the lack of collective training in formations; prolonged periods of contact with the enemy; the absence of adequate organisation to provide trained reinforcements; and the problem of malaria and the lack of resources. This was an astonishing catalogue of mismanagement but the disastrous first campaign in the Arakan had shown how dire the situation had become. The Committee recommended a number of proposals to benefit the welfare of the British and Indian troops and to improve morale. But most importantly it tried to improve the training situation through a thorough basic training of recruits followed by a period of jungle training and stressed the need for a central jungle warfare doctrine that this training could follow. Other recommendations included the ending of 'milking', increasing the pay of both the British and Indian infantry, improving the quality of officers and NCOs and of the reinforcement system. It stressed the importance of collective formation training, something which had not occurred before the First Arakan campaign, at which time training had only been undertaken up to battalion level. It also remarked on the need for more co-operation with other arms as well as the Royal Air Force. It concluded that few units could be described to be fully efficient in jungle warfare and that the new emphasis in training should be on jungle warfare and fighting rather than amphibious, desert or internal security training.

The new doctrine came with the publication of 80,000 copies of the fourth edition of Military Training Pamphlet No. 9 (India), *The Jungle Book*, in September 1943. It doubled the circulation of the previous editions and was produced to pass on the latest knowledge on jungle fighting to every officer and British NCO. It included lessons from Malaya, the retreat from Burma, the First Arakan campaign and from the Australian and American experiences of fighting the Japanese in the South-West Pacific Theatre. The new format included photographs and cartoons for the first time in order to make it more appealing to the men and to popularise training rather than using the usual dull training manuals.

These recommendations were put into practice by the new Commander-in-Chief India, General Sir Claude Auchinleck. The 14th and 39th Indian Divisions were designated as the new training divisions. The 14th Division which had been on the north-east frontier during 1942 and had fought at the First Arakan, was now based at Chhindwara in Madhya Pradesh. The 39th was at Saharanpur and, as 1st Burma Division, had been involved in the retreat from Burma and since then had been training for jungle warfare for six months. British infantry reinforcements were trained in jungle warfare by the new 52nd Brigade at Budni in Bhopal State, after a spell of basic training with the 13th Battalion, the Sherwood Foresters at Jubbulpore. The rest and reinforcement camps were reorganised under Colonel Gradige. Each camp was allocated to a particular division, realistic training was undertaken and the overall standard of discipline improved.

The new training divisions taught jungle warfare to the new soldiers. The 14th Indian Division started taking recruits from the beginning of December and the 52nd British Brigade by mid-December. The 14th Division's location was surrounded by jungle but the climate was comparatively mild, which meant that training could continue all year

British soldier sighting his 2in. mortar during training. (courtesy of the Trustees of the Imperial War Museum)

round. The division not only trained infantry but all arms, including British gunners, engineers and signallers. For the infantry the emphasis would be on section training, whereas the other arms would concentrate on weapons training. Recruits, including officers and NCOs, were trained at section and platoon level by a representative training battalion from their regiment within the training division.

The division was commanded by Major-general 'Tiger' Curtis who had served in both the retreat from Burma and the First Arakan. However, the Division had only a handful of other officers with battle experience against the Japanese and although some instructors were sent from serving battalions, units rarely sent their best men. It took three months to train the instructors.

Two soldiers hidden in the jungle armed with Rifle No. 1 Mark 3 and a Boys anti-tank rifle. (courtesy of the Trustees of the Imperial War Museum)

The training was intensive involving nine-hour days, six days a week including three nights' work a week. Recruits spent the first month in the camp training in battle drill, field movement and weapons training. The second month involved training in the jungle, living in trainee-made *bashas*, with numerous exercises using live ammunition. One exercise that helped introduce the troops to the noise of battle and accustom them to the supporting arms involved an advance of 250 yards towards an enemy-held *nullah*; 25-pdrs were used as the artillery support, with medium machine-gun fire from the flanks. Once they had reached the enemy lines, explosive charges were set off to simulate enemy artillery support for a counter-attack. In all exercises, there was strict discipline. Silence was maintained at all times, no litter was dropped and all ranks were stripped to the waist to aid acclimatisation, earning them the nickname 'the Bareback Division'. There were long patrols of between 36 and 48 hours and leaders were responsible for their troops' administrative needs and anti-malarial discipline. At the end of the two months, the trainees were expected to be able to march 25 miles a day with full equipment.

There were visits from serving officers to lecture on operational lessons from Burma and other experts such as Jim Corbett who taught jungle lore to the men of the training divisions. His book, *Man-Eaters of Kumaon,* was recommended reading in the training division. It described some of Corbett's experiences of tracking down tigers in the jungle. It was thought that valuable lessons of jungle lore could be learnt and then applied to operations against the Japanese. After two months the recruits were sent to a holding company where training was continued until they could join their battalions as reinforcements.

The Jungle Warfare School at Comilla was moved to Sevoke near Darjeeling in northern Bihar in 1943. The course lasted 15 days and the syllabus consisted of patrolling, living off the land, fire control, minor tactics, the preparation of road blocks and other obstacles, house-to-house fighting, camouflage, use of small craft, explosives, booby-traps and jungle lore. It finished with a three-day course in the jungle. Due to the demand for places on the course a second jungle warfare school was opened at Shimoga in November 1943. Lessons learnt at the schools were then taken back to the battalion to be put into practice. Individual and section training came first and then training at brigade and divisional level was undertaken. Leadership at junior officer level was essential in training as they would be the leaders in the jungle.

The 1st Battalion, Queen's Royal Regiment, joined the 7th Indian Division in December 1942 and together with the 4/1st Gurkhas and the 4/15th Punjabis made up 33rd Indian Infantry Brigade. Prior to this, despite the Japanese invasion, the battalion's training had been for open fighting suitable for the North-West Frontier and the Middle East. The division moved in January 1943 to the Chhindwara area, made famous by Rudyard Kipling's *Jungle Book*, to embark on training. The Division's training team was led by two veterans of the retreat from Burma, Lieutenant-Colonel Marindin and Captain Peacock. Peacock also had been a forest officer in Burma and he taught the men jungle lore such as how to eat rice, travel light, use camouflage and generally to 'make the jungle your friend'. For example, to achieve a distant view in primary jungle, a soldier should bend down and look along the ground, and if a soldier gets lost in the jungle the advice was to go downhill until he came upon a stream and follow it until he saw signs of native habitation. Peacock also showed the different uses of bamboo for eating, drinking, cooking, making rafts and *panjis*, sharpened bamboo stakes hidden in the ground for an ambush.

Troops were taught how to live off the land where rice, tea, sugar and salt were the main staples of diet. To this could be added the wildlife, fish, vegetables and fruit available in the jungle, and troops were taught which plants also had medicinal qualities. Section, platoon and company training for jungle warfare was undertaken. This meant physical fitness, night work, patrolling, weapon training, battle drills, compass work and map reading, anti-malarial discipline, hygiene, digging of weapon pits, river crossing and swimming, use of signals equipment and knowing your enemy. It was the first opportunity for the division to co-operate in a jungle environment with artillery, mortars and medium machine guns. By March the Division was taking part in inter-brigade exercises and then a month was spent training the whole division as a formation, ending up with a divisional exercise, 'Panther', which lasted 15 days. The main lessons learnt were patrolling, encirclement and to expect the unexpected in the jungle. At the end of April, infantry training was completed and the division's artillery component was reorganised with the arrival of one of the new jungle regiments, the 139th Jungle Field Regiment. One battery was equipped with 3.7in. howitzers and the other with 16 3in. mortars to give artillery support where the 25-pdrs could not be used. From May to July the division carried out training with these artillery regiments and the 25th Dragoons, Royal Armoured Corps.

Jungle training could be quite enjoyable as well as necessary. Major Gadsdon remembered his time at Chhindwara with 7th Indian Division in February 1943 as one of the best times in his army service:

> We were sent, on detachment, out into the wilds, to acclimatise to the jungle, and made camp by the river, with a deep rock pool in which to swim, every afternoon. At the age of 24 I commanded about three hundred men, miles from the nearest senior officer, and found it good.

Recruits for officer training who were to become emergency commissioned officers, that is, those enlisted for wartime service, came out to India and, whether they were in the British Army or the Indian Army, were trained for six months at the Officers' Training School at Mhow in central India and then joined a training division for jungle training.

Lee Medium Tanks of the 25th Dragoons. The tanks were originally constructed by the US Army as an infantry tank. (courtesy of the Trustees of the Imperial War Museum)

DAILY LIFE IN THE JUNGLE

Life in the jungle in the early stages of the war often had a depressing effect on the morale of British troops. This was addressed later in the war by measures such as keeping troops fully informed of the current situation and only holding them at the front for shorter periods of time. The strain of keeping alert meant that troops needed frequent rest, otherwise efficiency and morale would be affected. Thus, troops were relieved as often as possible. But due to the distances involved in the jungle this was not always feasible so rest areas were set up within one day's march of the front and units were intended to be in the rest area for two weeks out of every six. Here they would undergo a medical examination, rations would be increased and the unit reorganised.

The situation was helped by the fact that, later in the war, mail, newspapers and cigarettes were in abundant supply. Air supply was the answer to the previous long and tenuous lines of supply and the speedy air evacuation of some at least of the wounded improved morale dramatically. For instance, in the Arakan during 1942 it took an NCO and five bearers 17.5 hours to take two walking wounded and a stretcher from the first-aid post to a dressing station three miles away. There were also occasional visits by mobile cinemas and theatrical troupes, whose members found that the warmth of their welcome increased with every mile they went forward. The locally raised BESA (Bengal Entertainment for the Services Association), or 'Besa Belles' as they were known, was one group which toured many of the army camps.

Most British soldiers had no experience of the jungle. The silence, the limited vision, the slowness and difficulty of movement and the sense of isolation were unnerving. Soldiers had to overcome the permanent dampness, the dangers of disease and the jungle wildlife. For instance, leeches were inveterate pests in the jungle and in addition to the small

British troops playing cards, in a rest area in the jungle. (courtesy of the Trustees of the Imperial War Museum)

British troops constructing the road from India into Burma. The road passed through jungle, mountains and streams and took six months to build. (courtesy of the Trustees of the Imperial War Museum)

black leeches the yellow and green elephant leech was found in the pools on the fringes of the jungle. Soldiers soon learned that the most effective relief was removing them with burning cigarettes. The advent of the dry season meant that leeches were replaced by jungle ticks bearing scrub typhus.

Hygiene was of the utmost importance in the jungle. For instance, all excreta had to be buried immediately, drinking water was boiled or chlorinated and general common sense with regard to cleanliness helped prevent infection. The monsoon also meant the increase of the malarial mosquitoes, with malaria being the largest source of casualties. It reached epidemic proportions during the monsoon of 1942 in North–East India when whole units were laid low. As a result an anti-mosquito drill was introduced. All tents and shelters were sprayed before morning parade and all men were ordered to apply anti-mosquito cream before leaving the tent. At evening parade all men were inspected by the officer in charge to make sure the cream had been applied again and then the tents would be sprayed inside and out. Officers of troops who did not adhere to the drill were severely reprimanded. Long trousers with gaiters or puttees and long-sleeved tunics or shirts were worn to help guard against mosquito bites. In addition a medical jungle warfare school was instigated in July 1943. It was attended by all divisional officers based in North-East India. Medical advances meant that malaria could be contained through insecticides, anti-malarial discipline and mepacrine. In the forward areas, the disease was treated at Malarial Forward Treatment Units. This meant that there were now higher survival rates due to the decreased evacuation time and the unit and lines of communication were less affected by malaria casualties.

The rigour of daily life in the jungle meant that good levels of sustenance improved both morale and the effectiveness of troops fighting in the jungle, although Burma probably remained the worst theatre for food. Because of the heat, much of the tinned food was a congealed sludge by the time it reached the troops or it was infested with insects. The 48-hour mess-tin ration was standard for troops in action in the Far East until 1943 when it was replaced by the American 24-hour ration pack. In addition, an emergency ration tin was issued before offensives to be consumed only on orders from an officer. American K rations, again a box each for breakfast, dinner and supper, were also issued to British troops. The contents were fairly popular, particularly the American cigarettes, but, as with any rations, the monotony of eating the same foods day after day brought complaints from the soldiers. The biscuits in the packs were liked only by the Gurkhas and the insufficient quantity of American meat meant that British troops hankered after bully beef. But the real complaint was the lack of tea, seen as a great 'jungle sustainer'. British composite rations for troops out of action were split up and distributed between the platoon and section and consisted of six packets of biscuits, one tin of meat or Spam, one tin of cheese, a portion of sugar, two bars of chocolate, six small bags of tea, salt, matches, powdered milk, four packs of ten cigarettes (usually the unpopular Victory V cigarettes). These British rations would last one man for four days.

A typical day for a soldier in the jungle might begin with a wake-up call before daybreak. He probably hadn't had a good sleep for weeks, and then only in the cramped conditions of a two-feet-deep fox-hole, as 'stag' or sentry duty changed every four hours. The only form of cooking allowed was the morning 'brew' as it was smokeless, using a

British troops queuing up to draw their lunchtime rations, holding their mess tins and tin mugs. (courtesy of the Trustees of the Imperial War Museum)

tommy-cooker with petrol or meths as fuel. The most important event of the day was the arrival of the carrier, mule, motorised transport or plane ration columns bringing rations, the rum issue, mail and issues of SEAC. Once the rations had arrived the quartermaster distributed them to the companies, which in turn distributed them to platoons and sections. A fox-hole would usually have half a section commanded by a corporal or lance-corporal. The cooking consisted of crumbling biscuits into hot water and stirring in milk and sugar to make porridge together with the inevitable bully beef, all washed down with hot tea.

Shaving in the jungle was not always possible but beards could attract insects and jungle sores. Soldiers were generally careful to wash their feet and change their socks regularly but not the rest of the body as water might be limited and they would not have clean clothes to put on. Rifles had to be cleaned every day with oil and 'four-by-two' (a cleaning rag), especially in the monsoon as rust would build up.

There were two methods of overcoming the fear encountered in the jungle, through training and experience, of which training was vitally important.

British troops enjoying a recently opened 'Lounge' for the forces at Bangalore in Mysore. The notice sets out the amenities and comforts provided by the new 'Lounge' club. (courtesy of the Trustees of the Imperial War Museum)

APPEARANCE AND EQUIPMENT

In Malaya and Burma in 1941–42, troops wore standard tropical kit called khaki drill (KD), a term which originated from a combination of the old Urdu word *khak* meaning dust and the fact that the uniform was made from a 'drilled' cotton fabric. It had been standard dress throughout the empire since 1896, consisting of shirts, shorts and puttees together with the Wolsey pattern or Indian pattern helmet for troops serving in hot climates. However, the colour of KD and the use of shorts in the jungle were obviously unsuitable; shorts exposed legs to insect bites and stings, leading to malaria and other diseases. Early innovators such as Stewart in Malaya made his Argylls wear long trousers to counteract the danger but they were an exception at this early stage of the war. After the fall of Singapore and the retreat from Burma, the troops dyed their KD uniform and web equipment a dark green colour as more appropriate for wearing in the jungle, and bush hats or Australian slouch hats replaced both the Wolsey helmet and the tin helmet. Private Daniels remembered his first day in his training camp in India:

A Naik (Corporal) wearing the old uniform of khaki drill next to a British soldier in the new jungle-green uniform. (courtesy of the Trustees of the Imperial War Museum)

> Most of the day was spent getting straight my 'bunk' and changing kit for 'jungle green'. The tunic shirt with four pockets was green, also the trousers which were long ones (no shorts), these tucked into gaiters which were canvas with straps and buckle instead of short puttees. Our equipment that had been scrubbed white for our service in Persia and Iraq now had to be dyed green, this was done by putting into a large vat of boiling green dye – our underclothes were also dyed green – we were issued with Australian type bush hats on which we had to sew our divisional sign.

After KD stocks were used up, Indian-made jungle-green uniform was issued in 1943, consisting of Aertex battle dress shirt, trousers and bush jacket, and was generally worn by all the British and Commonwealth armies until 1945. Soldiers were issued with two shirts, two pairs of trousers, puttees and boots. The high humidity in the jungle tended to rot fabric and leather quickly and standard-issue army boots disintegrated in about ten days in the jungle. Lightweight canvas and rubber boots were preferred for patrolling but were not very robust and were eventually replaced by American jungle boots. Troops also wore captured Japanese jungle boots in preference to British boots as they had thick crêpe soles. The jungle even rotted the cord for the identity tags and the fibre identity discs often lost their markings in the heat. The cord was often replaced with a metal chain and later in the war rot-proof nylon cord was issued. The fibre tags were later replaced with stainless steel ones in the British Army and aluminium discs were adopted in India.

Troops in the jungle were often at the end of very long and difficult supply lines and therefore needed enough equipment to be self-sufficient for short periods in between resupplies. Their haversacks contained the following: cutlery, mug, mess tin, emergency ration pack, towel, wash kit, socks, pullover, cape, stove, mosquito cream and rations. A soldier would also carry spare clothing to prevent the chafing caused by wet clothing as well as the ubiquitous 'housewife', mosquito net, blanket and steel helmet. Loads were meant to be 40lbs or lighter but with the addition of weapons and web equipment they were usually heavier.

In June 1943, 202 Military Mission under Major-General J. S. Lethbridge, otherwise known as the Lethbridge Mission, began a tour of the south-west Pacific, New Guinea and Burma, as well as India, Australia, New Zealand and America, in order to research equipment and organisation needed to defeat the Japanese. The resulting report published in March 1944 recommended, for instance, the replacement of the 1937 webbing which was generally thought of as clumsy and uncomfortable in the jungle. The braces chafed collars and armpits and dragged on the shoulders, particularly if wet, and could also attract mould. The recommended webbing was meant to address these problems as it would be lighter, rot-proof and with anti-corrosion metal fittings with an aluminium water bottle. The Mills Equipment Company designed new web equipment in early 1944, which was a single unit with larger pouches and 3in. shoulder bands. The bands were fixed to the pouches and crossed over at the back to prevent drag. Thus there was no need to tighten the belt and this increased comfort and ventilation. Inside the back of the haversack and the pack was a lining of oiled cotton cloth to stop perspiration penetrating to the webbing. After modification this design was adopted for the 1944 pattern web equipment, but was not actually in service before the end of the war. The uniform adopted was a copy of the US Army field uniform with Aertex being replaced by 'olive green' drill for the jacket and trousers. Similarly, other items were designed specifically for the Far East, such as mosquito nets for head and hands, lightweight blankets, jungle-green puttees and canvas and rubber jungle boots, again based on the American issue. However, the Lethbridge recommendations were only really put into practice for British troops earmarked to go out to the Far East after the victory in Europe.

WEAPONS

The Argylls were fairly well equipped for a unit in Malaya. They had the use of four Lanchester armoured cars, each equipped with two .303in. Vickers machine guns and one .5in. machine gun, supposed to be effective against light armour, as well as three South African Marmons, each with one Vickers and an anti-tank rifle. In addition, the battalion had four 3in. and a few 2in. mortars. Each patrol was given a Thompson sub-machine gun as an alternative to the Sten, which, although useful for close-quarter fighting in the jungle, was prone to jamming and its 9mm round was a little less effective.

In Burma, British battalions were seriously under-equipped. In 1940 the Burma office had requested modern weapons but had been refused due to the shortage of Bren guns and mortars; thus issue to Burma would not be justifiable. All that could be spared were two Bren guns per battalion when four Brens, two anti-tank rifles, two 2in. mortars and two 3in. mortars had been the minimum requested. The disaster at Sittang Bridge sealed the fate of the troops in Burma. Obsolete equipment was used at Sittang, such as the World War I vintage 18-pdr guns and Lewis guns as anti-aircraft guns. After Sittang Bridge the infantrymen were never properly equipped for the remainder of the retreat from Burma; 17th Indian Division was down to 1,420 rifles, 56 Bren guns and 68 Thompson sub-machine guns.

Lessons learned from the Burma campaign showed that some equipment was particularly important in the jungle. For example, mortars, which became the main support weapon of the infantryman in the jungle. The portability of the 2in. mortar and the range of the more bulky 3in. mortars were highly valued as their concentrated fire power could be devastating, particularly when the enemy had not had time to dig deep. Modifications were made to adapt these weapons for jungle conditions: the 3in. mortar's baseplate was strengthened and a new sight installed to increase the range to 2,750 yards for the Mark 4 version. The Mark 5 was a specially designed lighter version for use in the Far East, but only 5,000 had been produced by the end of the war. The 2in. was fitted with a 'bowed' plate to reduce its weight from 19 to 11lbs but without effecting its accuracy and range.

Private Gumbrell of the 1st Battalion, Queen's Royal Regiment, was transferred to the jungle battle school at Ranchi for 2in. mortar training. He commented that:

My 2in. mortar was a superb weapon and although it was meant to be fired with an elongated base plate attached, we found out that it could be held on the right-hand thigh with left leg in kneeling posture. It had to be held quite firmly for fear of bruising or muscle injury to the thigh. Personal involvement of this fine weapon allowed me to concentrate on a very highly sophisticated method of range-finding so that my projectile would land within the target area.

Later in the war, after the initial rejection of anti-tank weapons such as the .55-in. Boys rifle by the British infantryman for fighting in the jungle, the PIAT

Troops of the Manchester Regiment cleaning their weapons. The soldier on the left is cleaning his 2in. mortar, while the other two in the foreground are cleaning a Mark 2 Bren gun and a Sten gun Mark 2, and the soldier in the background is cleaning his No. 2 Mark 1 Enfield revolver. (courtesy of the Trustees of the Imperial War Museum)

(Projector, Infantry, Anti-tank) was particularly effective against the entrenched Japanese bunkers.

The *dhah*, an Indian knife used in the Burma campaigns for clearing jungle undergrowth, was seen as essential even though it was an encumbrance.

Other infantry weapons that proved particularly effective in the jungle included grenades such as the No. 36 grenade or Mills bomb and the plastic '77' which was a smoke grenade used for clearing bunkers and that was kept in one pouch of the webbing. Bren guns and medium machine guns were used for covering fire. Two Bren gun magazines were kept in another pouch and could be used either for the Bren or a light machine gun. The Bren gunner usually fired lying down with another soldier on hand to change the magazine. The Bren could also be fired from the hip. One other weapon privately purchased but often carried by infantrymen was a flick-knife bought in Indian bazaars.

In 1939 infantrymen were armed with the Short Magazine Lee Enfield .303in. Mark 3 pattern. The Mark 4 was issued to front-line troops in Europe by 1942 but few were in service in the Far East before 1944. India Command undertook further research into infantry rifles in order to make them smaller and lighter for easier handling in the jungle. The result was the precursor to the No. 5 Jungle Carbine, which was officially adopted by the War Office in September 1944, but was actually developed in India in 1943, though the project was cancelled and very few were produced at the time. The No. 5 Mark 1 was 5in. shorter and 2lbs lighter in order to make it easier to manoeuvre in the jungle. However, the No. 5 was not popular with the soldiers due to the excessive recoil and its inaccuracy and was declared obsolete in 1947.

3.7in. howitzer in action in Burma. This howitzer was originally developed for the Indian Mountain Artillery. It was particularly useful in the jungle as it could be quickly dismantled for transport by mule or by manpower. (courtesy of the Trustees of the Imperial War Museum)

TACTICS

Most troops in Malaya were not well trained, particularly in jungle warfare, but there were successful actions against the Japanese. The Argylls' first action in Malaya at the battle of Grik Road showed the importance of jungle training. The Argylls defended in depth and undertook aggressive encircling patrols. When they took Sumpitan, the battalion had advanced 36 miles in five hours. Stewart noted that when the Japanese were attacked they bunched. When the Argylls finally had to withdraw due to the weight of Japanese forces, it was again a fighting withdrawal using ambushes and encirclement. The 12th Indian Infantry Brigade's delaying tactics at Kampar allowed the rest of 11th Indian Division to retreat back into central Malaya and regroup. However, Stewart did not always get his tactics correct: at the battle of Slim river on 7 January 1942 his brigade (he was by now in command of 12th Brigade), exhausted and depleted due to bad positioning and the lack of anti-tank weapons and anti-tank mines, could not prevent the Japanese tanks from using the main road to smash right through the brigade. His tactics of filleting had been shown to be successful – but on this occasion by the enemy.

25-pdr in action. The 25-pdr was developed during the 1930s and was in production by 1940. It could fire high- explosive, smoke and armour-piercing shells. These guns were also modified for the jungle by shortening the axle length in order to improve movement. (courtesy of the Trustees of the Imperial War Museum)

After the defeats in Burma and Malaya there was much reorganisation. As a new Inspector of Infantry, Major-General Reginald Savory, who had commanded 23rd Indian Division in Assam, was appointed to address the problem of infantry training. Other appointments included a new Inspector of Training Centres and a new Director of Military Training, in April and May of 1943 respectively. Higher up the chain of command, General Sir Claude Auchinleck replaced General Wavell as Commander-in-Chief India, Wavell becoming Viceroy of India while Lord Louis Mountbatten was appointed Supreme Allied Commander, SEAC. Operational duties were devolved from India Command who now had more opportunity to concentrate on training and doctrine. At the same time, General Slim became commander of 14th Army and he made sure that training was at the top of the agenda for the formations under his command.

Operations in Burma and Malaya had shown the importance of junior leaders, as command must be decentralised in the jungle and therefore junior officers had to make instant decisions without recourse to the chain of command. This came through training and practical experience. Other lessons included the necessity of patrolling. There were two types of patrol, 'reconnaissance', which consisted of not more than six men, and 'fighting', where the minimum was platoon strength. The fighting patrol was often organised into three manoeuvre sections and one support section, the latter armed with 2in. mortars, rifle grenades and two light machine guns. Troops were encouraged not to leave litter on patrol and movement was off the tracks so as not to give intelligence to the enemy.

During an attack in the jungle, the attacker has the advantage through intelligence and previous patrolling, and has the element of surprise. Thus, the frontal approach was usually discounted in favour of encirclement and flanking movements. The attacking force would be divided into four components (see plates D and E). The first element fixes the track or some tactical feature and fixes the enemy. The second and third outflank one or both of the enemy's flanks or even the rear of the enemy. The fourth component was the reserve, which would exploit the success of the flanking movement or be able to contain the enemy counterattack. Similar tactics had proved effective when used by the Japanese in their advance through Malaya and Burma. Therefore, troops needed to counter-attack immediately after Japanese infiltration and before the enemy could build up its forces.

The Japanese were equally determined in defence, with their use of the supporting defensive bunker system. In the First Arakan campaign, the bunkers at Donbaik were very difficult to destroy as they were skilfully sited, carefully camouflaged and strongly built and seemed to be indestructible. Each normally consisted of a small heavily fortified post of about ten men who were positioned to protect a neighbouring bunker. The two strongest bunkers at Donbaik were named 'S4' and 'S5' and were linked by interconnecting positions. S5 was a hollowed-out mound on a dry water-course, making it almost invisible to the attacking British forces. Shelling did inflict casualties in the bunkers, and as a result the Japanese left one sentry in the bunker while the rest of the platoon hid in nearby caves during Allied bombardments. Once the shelling ceased the Japanese would occupy the bunker to repel the imminent attack. On 1 February 1942 during the First Arakan campaign a whole brigade plus eight Valentine tanks, one and a half field batteries and a light anti-aircraft battery attacked the S4 and S5 bunker positions and failed. The tanks were completely wasted as there had been no previous training with armour, they had arrived only the night before and three were ditched at the beginning of the assault. The artillery support was inadequate with no rolling barrages or smoke screens against a well-dug-in enemy. There was, moreover, little co-operation between infantry and artillery. As elsewhere at this time, infantry attacks started late and therefore could not take full advantage of the covering artillery fire, giving the Japanese time to man their fire positions to repel the attacks. In fact, Allied tactics during the First Arakan seemed to be one-dimensional, consisting of artillery barrages followed by the infantry going forward. Even when Brigadier Cavendish of 6th Brigade proposed a surprise attack, it was still preceded by an artillery barrage.

Training

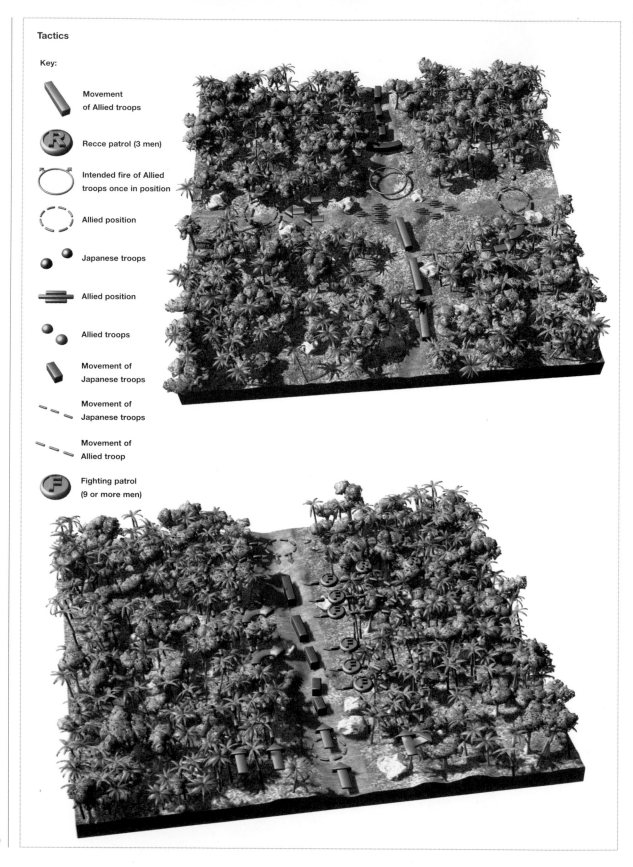

Tactics

Key:

	Movement of Allied troops
(R)	Recce patrol (3 men)
◯	Intended fire of Allied troops once in position
◌	Allied position
• ●	Japanese troops
▭	Allied position
• ●	Allied troops
▭	Movement of Japanese troops
– – –	Movement of Japanese troops
– – –	Movement of Allied troop
(F)	Fighting patrol (9 or more men)

D

Ambush

Key:
(symbols also as key for Plate D)

 Three Allied troops with light machine guns

 Position of Allied troops

 Mortar fire

 Possible position of Japanese troops

 Intended mortar-fire zone

Weapons

1

2

3

4

5

6

7

8

9

F

Badges and formation signs

1

2

3

4

5

6

7

8

9

10

11

12

13

14

15

16

17

18

19

20

G

Soldier, 1st Battalion, Queen's Royal Regiment

H

New tactics were needed to counteract these extremely strong defences. The infantry had to co-operate with other arms, such as artillery, tanks and air support, as well as to maximise their own resources such as the PIAT. A system was drawn up to destroy these defensive positions. First, the reconnaissance of the enemy position would be undertaken by infantry patrols. The bunker and the surrounding area would then be bombarded by artillery, tanks or air bombardment. The attack itself would consist of infantry supported by tanks, machine guns and 6-pdr anti-tank guns which were quite effective at bunker-busting. Movement was indicated by the leading infantry by throwing down No. 77 smoke grenades every five or ten minutes so that the supporting arms could adjust their fire. In addition, 25-pdr, 3.7in. howitzers and 3-inch mortars would fire smoke as well as high-explosive shells as the infantry approached the objective, giving them cover from the defences. Tanks, once they were at a reasonably close range, would use solid shot to loosen the Japanese bunkers, then switch to high-explosive shells to burst inside the bunkers. When the tanks were within 100 to 300 yards, they switched to machine guns to allow the infantry to advance without the threat of shell splinters. The infantry would then advance to within 15 yards of a Japanese position before attacking with grenades and bayonets. The tanks could also help out with the immediate counter-attack, by changing to 75mm armour-piercing shells to give more support to the infantry and loosen the supports of the bunker before the enemy was able to return there. Finally, another wave of infantry was usually sent in to mop up and deal with a counter-attack.

Lieutenant-General Noel Irwin talking to Indian troops in the forward areas in Burma. Irwin was Eastern Army Commander until the debacle at the First Arakan when he was replaced by General Giffard, a veteran of the bush war in East Africa during World War I. (courtesy of the Trustees of the Imperial War Museum)

A jungle patrol attacks a native *basha* in a banana grove. (courtesy of the Trustees of the Imperial War Museum)

New tactics were also needed in defenc since it was impossible for a static defensive line to fend off a jungle attack. The actual defensive position was ideally a series of mutually supporting posts which in the jungle could be quite close together. Automatic weapons were essential for this mutual support because artillery was not always available. The posts also had to be self-contained, with sufficient water and supplies for several days, and had to make the most of available natural obstacles and camouflage. In addition, posts could be defended by ground and tree snipers. Snipers, patrols and listening posts combined would help prevent enemy infiltration, but also essential was a central reserve, ready to attack immediately, and mortars ready to shoot into areas the enemy might infiltrate. The most important element of the defence was aggression.

Ambushes were used in both defence and attack. *Panji* sticks were most effective and were placed parallel to or just off the track so that the Japanese scattering after the ambush would find themselves impaled. The Allies found this method was particularly successful. The Japanese also had ruses in ambushes for instance, they often feigned death for long periods of time so that they could surprise unsuspecting Allied troops

ON CAMPAIGN

The west tunnel on the Maungdaw–Buthidaung road (circled) looking towards Maungdaw on the Naaf river estuary, just visible in the distance. (courtesy of the Trustees of the Imperial War Museum)

The 1st Battalion, Queen's Royal Regiment, of 7th Indian Division was earmarked for the Second Arakan campaign in August 1943. The Arakan peninsula was divided by the Mayu range with the Mayu valley to the east and the Bay of Bengal on the west. The peninsula was covered with very dense jungle with few tracks, which became almost impassable during the monsoon season of June to September. The battalion arrived in Chittagong on 11 September and entrained for Doharzi from where they had a five-day march to the Brigade Camp at Pondiywa at the head of the Naaf river. It was still the monsoon season, so supply lines were very difficult as the roads were often impassable. *Sampans* could be used up the river and supplies had then to be carried on mules through the jungle to the camp. The brigade was in reserve while the remainder of the division went up to the front. Training was carried out even this near to the front, for example, in the handling of the unfamiliar *sampans*. In contrast to the First Arakan, troops were allowed to acclimatise themselves to the jungle and gain confidence through patrolling. On 30 September Major G. S. Grimston took over command of the battalion and B Company of the Queen's was commanded by Captain M. A. Lowry. The first action for B Company was to carry out a diversionary attack against Maungdaw by bombarding various targets with their 3in. mortars. The unit moved up the Teknaf River in 18 *sampans* and one larger craft carrying the mortars and their crews. The force arrived at midnight at the beachhead, which was then held by one

42

platoon, and the mortars and their crews were in position by 11.30 am. The bombardment was fired and no enemy was encountered. On 10 November the Queen's Royal Regiment handed over the Teknaf peninsula to the 4th Rajputs of 5th Indian Division.

The Queen's Royal Regiment moved to Garret's Garden Camp on Goppe Pass and was again in reserve undertaking jungle training. On 26 November the battalion marched over the pass towards the front line. In B Company's first fighting patrol the objective was to discover if there were any enemy troops in the Ngakragyaung area and, if not, to take possession of the hill and Point 206. B and C Companies set off at 8.00pm on 1 December and had to cross paddy fields flooded waist-high. As they passed the outskirts of Ngakragyaung village they heard voices and realised that the Japanese were near the village. They flanked it and found out that it was supported by a machine-gun post and two or three light machine guns. The fire discipline of the company was maintained, whereas, in contrast, the Japanese troops panicked. Captain Lowry withdrew B Company as the reconnaissance had been successful and there was no need for unnecessary casualties. C Company got to Point 206 without opposition and were ordered to withdraw. However, they had to make a fighting withdrawal due to a Japanese counter-attack. The patrol had been successful in bringing back valuable intelligence and there were no casualties. Generally two patrols, like this one, were sent out every day, with a fighting patrol sent out every other day and an ambush patrol was taken alternatively with another company. Even in a

Mules carrying ammunition and water supplies to troops on the Arakan Front. (courtesy of the Trustees of the Imperial War Museum)

relatively quiet sector troops had little chance to rest and these small-scale encounters with the enemy helped build confidence and eliminate the myth of the Japanese 'supermen' in the jungle.

The Queen's Royal Regiment were relieved on 3 December and Lieutenant-Colonel H. G. Duncombe took over command of the battalion while Major Grimston reverted to Second-in-Command. The next objective for the Queen's Royal Regiment was the capture of Point 182. On 18 December B Company advanced to the hills south and east of Point 182 to protect the start line for a D Company attack after a heavy artillery barrage. B Company reached its objective on time, 8.30am. D Company passed through B Company to mount their attack. However, the going was so steep that it took them until midday to reach the top, and well-dug-in Japanese defenders with machine guns were covering the tracks. D Company feinted a frontal attack by one platoon while another went around the flank and in the surprise attack completely defeated the enemy, who were then fired on by B Company in their flight. One of the wounded was brought in as a prisoner, the first taken in 7th Indian Division. The Queen's Royal Regiment dug in for the inevitable counter-attack. The leading Japanese soldier came within ten yards of the commanding officer, Lieutenant-Colonel H. G. Duncombe, who managed to throw a grenade, but a bombing party counter-attack led by Major Grimston retook the Battalion HQ.

The 7th Indian Division's objective was to advance towards and take Buthidaung and Ledwedet fortress down the west side of the Mayu Ridge, with the 5th Indian Division advancing down the east side to take Maungdaw and the Razabil fortress, while the 81st West African Division was to advance down the Kaladan valley to prevent a Japanese counter-attack. 7th Division's plan was for 33rd Brigade to cut the Buthidaung tunnels near Ledwedet village allowing 89th Brigade and the 25th Dragoons with its tanks to break through to Buthidaung isolating the Ledwedet fortress. The other brigade of the Division, 114th, was to cut the Buthiduang–Ratheduang road and prevent the defending enemy troops at Buthidaung from escaping.

B Company spent Christmas moving forward as the lead company, advancing to the hills overlooking the Ledwedet Chaung. As it was Christmas the men were permitted a number of small fires were allowed on which to brew tea and available officers went to Battalion HQ for a Christmas toast. The Japanese, who were about 300 yards away, played gramophone records, including 'Home Sweet Home'. The next day Christmas was celebrated with BESA putting on two performances at Battalion HQ and the troops were given a Christmas meal of duck, peas, plum pudding, cakes and beer. There was also a carol service the day after.

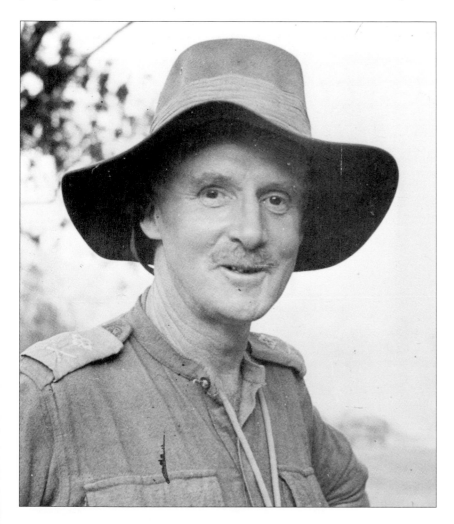

Major-General Frank Messervy, who took over command of 7th Indian Division from Major-General Corbett. He served with an Indian cavalry regiment, Hodson's Horse, during World War I. During World War II he had previously commanded Gazelle Force in Eritrea, 4th Indian Division and 7th Armoured Division (Desert Rats) in the Western Desert and was well known for his escape from the Germans by impersonating an old soldier. He was nicknamed 'General Frank' by the soldiers of 7th Division. (courtesy of the Trustees of the Imperial War Museum)

Sinzweya, also called the 'Admin Box'. (courtesy of the Trustees of the Imperial War Museum)

1 One Company, 2nd Battalion, West Yorkshire Regiment and Salvage Units.
2 Section 8 (Heavy) Anti-Aircraft Regiment, Royal Artillery.
3 Pattison's Post, supply depot and two supply issue sections.
4 Pattison's Post consisted of 62nd, 77th, 421st Field Companies, Indian Engineers, BORs of the West Yorkshire Regiment, 114 brigade staff, engineer HQ staff, army service and signals personnel and a mortar detachment.
5 20 Anti-Tank Company (Mule).
6 Ordnance Field Park.
7 Part of B Echelon, 89th Brigade.
8 One troop, 284th Anti-Tank Battery and RAF details.
9 Part of B Echelon, 89 Brigade.
10 B Echelon, 33rd Brigade.
11 4/8th Gurkha Rifles (at first less two companies); HQ 491 Light Anti-Aircraft Battery.
12 2nd King's Own Scottish Borderers (after 14 February) less two companies. Garrison reserve.
13 7th Division workshops.
13a HQ 89th Brigade (after 14 February).
1 Bridging lorries outside the defended area.
2 7/2nd Punjabis, less one company (after 11 February).
3 B Echelon, Divisional Signals, one section Motor Transport Officers' shop.

4 B Echelon, 136 and 139 Regiments, Royal Artillery.
5 284 Battery (24 Anti-Aircraft/Anti-Tank), less two troops.
18a. Extemporised Mortar Troop and HQ. 205 Battery (24 Anti-Aircraft/Anti-Tank).
1 8 and 65 Mule Companies, and Mobile Veterinary Section.
2 B Echelon 9th Brigade.
3 HQ 24 Mountain Regiment, Indian Artillery, and one section.
4 7th Division HQ, 9th HQ, Garrison HQ, 24 Anti-Aircraft/Anti-Tank Regiment.
5 Reinforcements 1 Queen's and 2 King's Own Scottish Borderers (original site of MDS – Main Dressing Station).
6 V Force Detachments (escaped from Taung).
7 MDS.
8 Rear 7th Division HQ.
9 HQ 2 West Yorkshire and Garrison reserve of Infantry. Two companies. 2 West Yorkshire till 15 February. Two companies. 2 King's Own Scottish Borderers added after 15 February.
10 One Squadron, 25th Dragoons. One Platoon 3/4th Bombay Grenadiers.
11 One Troop 205 Battery (24 Anti-Aircraft/Anti-Tank).
12 Ammunition Hill.
13 25th Dragoons, less two squadrons. A Companies, 3/4th Bombay Grenadiers, less one platoon.
14 6th Medium Regiment, Royal Artillery, less one battery. Mortar Battery, 139th Jungle Field Regiment.

The next objective for the Queen's Royal Regiment was to reconnoitre south of Ledwedet Chaung and to patrol Hill 162. On 9 January 17 Platoon under Lieutenant Halfhide was ordered to support an attack by the 1/4th Gurkhas by giving supporting fire from a flanking hill. The Platoon crossed the Ledwedet Chaung by swimming but came under heavy fire, which was countered by the Battalion's 3in. mortars. They reached the position and dug in, only to be bombarded by the Japanese artillery and mortars, but they kept on the position, again supported by the 3in. mortars. The Gurkhas' attack went ahead without any interference from this flank, after which 17 Platoon was able to withdraw. The enemy bombardment had been so intense that the equipment left on the surrounding ground was shot to pieces, but the quick dig in meant that the Platoon suffered only two casualties.

By the end of January, Maungdaw had been occupied and the road west of the Massif had been cut by 33rd Brigade. The battalion was meant to be replaced by the King's Own Scottish Borderers but this was delayed by the Japanese offensive, Operation HA-GO, whose aim was to draw Allied troops into the Arakan to create a diversion for the main Japanese advance towards the Imphal Plain. The plan was for the 55th Japanese Division to outflank the 7th Indian Division and then split the 7th and 5th Indian Divisions apart, destroying each in turn. The Japanese advance on 4 February 1944 was swift and Major-General Messervy's Divisional Headquarters at Launggyaung was overrun on 6 February, causing a breakdown in communications. He and the rest of his HQ managed to get back to the administrative area at Sinzweya, later called the 'Admin Box'. This meant that the Ngakyedauk pass (known as the 'Oke-Doke Pass' by the troops) was cut off and 33rd Brigade isolated, but formed a defensive 'box'. On 7 February a mortar battery was attacked in Wet valley, C Company was despatched to relieve the battery but was split up during the night and the one party under Captain G. K. P. Tattershall and the survivors of the battery managed to fight their way up the valley into the Admin Box. A Company became Brigade reserve and the other two companies formed Braganza Box around Battalion HQ. The companies in the Braganza Box aggressively patrolled the area but had little contact with the enemy as most of the fighting took place behind the box. A Company attacked the enemy with tank support on a number of occasions and on 22 February the company imposed a heavy defeat on the Japanese. The company rejoined the battalion on 28 February.

Maintaining the defensive boxes was only possible through the supplies dropped by the Royal Air Force, otherwise another withdrawal would have taken place. Instead the British and Indian Armies imposed the first defeat on the Japanese in the jungle through the use of aggressively defended localities supplied by air. The Battalion was relieved on 29 February and returned to Wet valley and there were no patrols for the first time in three months. The Queen's Royal Regiment were back in action on 7 March in order to follow up the Japanese defeat, and took Cain Hill south of the Maungdaw–Buthidaung road, supported by the whole divisional artillery.

After the important victories in the Arakan, both the 5th and the 7th Indian Divisions were transferred to the Imphal front. The Japanese Operation U-GO was aimed at the speedy capture of Imphal to forestall the imminent Allied invasion of Burma. The Japanese 31st Division's objective was the capture of Kohima to cut the supply route between

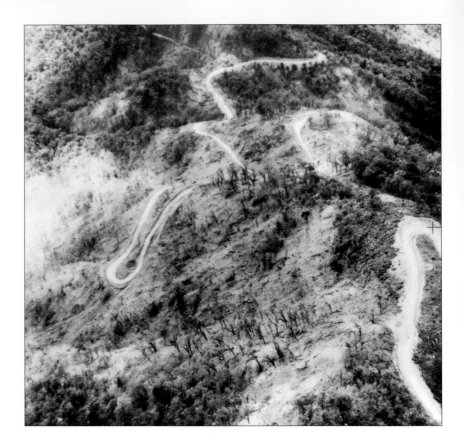

Dimapur and Imphal. The Kohima area was less densely covered by jungle than the previous battleground in the Arakan. The town was 5,000 feet above sea level surrounded by cultivated and terraced slopes in the immediate vicinity, with jungle-clad hills further away. Immediately, 161st Brigade of 5th Indian Division was sent into action with the 4th Royal West Kent Regiment, a battery of the 24th Mountain Regiment and the 2nd Field Company Royal Engineers joining the garrison at Kohima, which was mainly manned by non-combatant troops except for the Burma Regiment and the paramilitary Assam Rifles, and a battalion of the Assam Regiment. The rest of 161st Brigade were two miles away providing protection for the decisive artillery support from Jotsoma. Together they all survived the onslaught of a Japanese force of divisional strength for two weeks until relieved by the 2nd British Division, under the command of Major-General John Grover.

After this initial victory at Kohima, every hill and ridge had to be captured from the defending Japanese. One such action was the taking of Jail Hill by the 1st Battalion of the Queen's Royal Regiment of 33rd Brigade. They had been airlifted to Kohima on 8 April, after leaving the Admin Box on 3 April. The Queen's Royal Regiment was detached from its brigade and was responsible for protecting the railway line to Dimapur. Even in the midst of this action the battalion managed to find time for sporting competitions that also helped build unit morale. For instance, on 4 May, 10 Platoon beat Motor Transport Platoon in the final of the inter-platoon basketball competition. Lieutenant-Colonel Duncombe presented the winners with a tin of fruit, jam, milk, soap, a bottle of squash and 100 cigarettes to each of the players. Concerts were also produced by the

Engineer dump at Kohima during the monsoon in 1944. In the distance is Field Supply Depot (FSD) Hill and to the right is Garrison Hill. (courtesy of the Trustees of the Imperial War Museum)

battalion and B Company saw one just before being ordered to return to their brigade on 5 May, which now came under the command of 2nd Division. They debussed at Milestone 42 and climbed up the rifle range area of GPT (General Purpose Transport) Ridge. The battalion was ordered to attempt to take Jail Hill, one of the largest features in central Kohima. Although no reconnaissance of the objective had been undertaken, it was realised that the plan depended on the well-defended GPT Ridge being cleared. The attack was to be in two parts: (1); the capture of Pimple Hill by C Company after an artillery barrage, which then lifted to Jail Hill; (2); D Company was then to pass through C Company and attack Jail Hill when the barrage had finished. A Company was to follow up the attack and B Company was in reserve. The other two battalions of the brigade, together with a battalion of the Royal Scots, would clear GPT Ridge.

Continual rain on the preceding night had made the going very tough for the advancing infantry, making visability difficult and hampering forward movement. The Gurkhas and the Scots tried PIATs, 2-inch smoke mortars, bazookas and grenades but came under attack from GPT Ridge. It was now clear that Jail Hill could not be taken unless GPT Ridge and DIS Hill had also been taken. In addition tanks could not be brought in due to the weather. The battalion withdrew under artillery and mortar smoke. Lieutenant-Colonel Duncombe visited B Company the next day to inform the unit that the attack was not a failure as the battalion had captured its objectives even though the flanks were unprotected. He stated that he had ordered the withdrawal without recourse to higher command and the divisional commander had called it a gallant effort.

Kohima battlefield:

1 Deputy Commissioner's bungalow and tennis court.
2 Garrison Hill.
3 Kuki Piquet.
4 FSD Hill.
5 DIS Hill.
6 Jail Hill.
7 Road to Imphal.
8 Pimple Hill.
9 Congress Hill.
10 GPT Ridge.
11 Norfolk Ridge.
12 Rifle Range.
13 Two Tree Hill.
14 Jetsome Track.
15 Pulebadze Peak (7,532 feet).
16 South end of Pulebadze Ridge.
17 Top end of Aradura Spur.
18 Japvo Peak (9,890 feet).

OPPOSITE Map of Jail Hill and the surrounding hills taken by the 1st Battalion Queens Royal Regiment. (Courtesy of the Trustees of the Imperial War Museum)

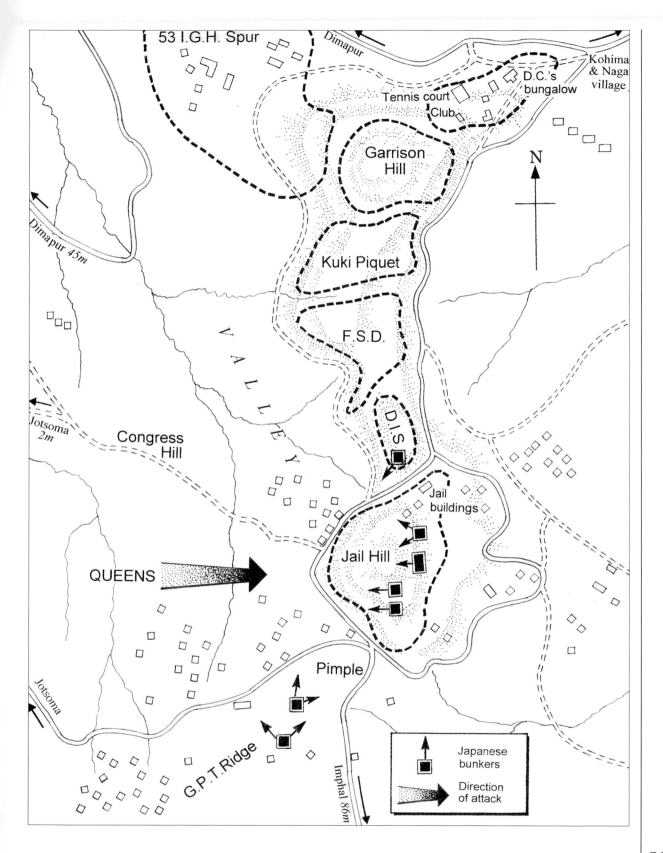

53 I.G.H. Spur

Dimapur

Kohima & Naga village

D.C.'s bungalow

Tennis court
Club

Garrison Hill

N

Dimapur 45m

Kuki Piquet

F.S.D.

Jotsoma 2m

Congress Hill

VALLEY

D.I.S.

Jail buildings

Jail Hill

QUEENS

Jotsoma

Pimple

G.P.T. Ridge

Imphal 86m

Japanese bunkers

Direction of attack

An artist's impression of a bunker on DIS Hill. (courtesy of the Trustees of the Imperial War Museum)

A new plan was drawn up for another attack by the whole brigade as part of a divisional objective to clear the central hills of Kohima. GPT Ridge was to be captured by another brigade and then the Queen's was to attack Jail Hill at first light and the 4/15th Punjabis were to capture DIS Hill, while the 1/1st Punjabis were to capture Pimple the night before and then dig in. The Queen's plan was for C and B Companies to attack the right and left of Jail Hill respectively with A and D Companies following up. Jail Hill and DIS Hill were to be bombarded by 25-lbs and 3 in. mortars, support would come from divisional machine guns. Tanks were to fire on the west side of Jail Hill and also help further if needed. Two bunker destroying parties of the Indian Engineers were also available. For B Company's attack 11 Platoon was on the right, with tactical HQ with Major Lowry in the centre, 10 Platoon on the right and 12 Platoon behind.

For the attack the troops were given one day's ration and strict water discipline was maintained. Troops were to carry an extra five rounds of tracer to indicate targets to tanks. Packs were left at the start line and the rum issue was at the forming-up position. The regimental aid post was positioned between Pimple and the main road and casualties could be evacuated by stretcher or jeep to the advanced dressing station. Before B Company's attack they were shelled and suffered a number of casualties.

The attack took place on 11 May, the battalion advancing under cover of darkness with heavy machine gun and artillery support. B Company got to the forming-up position at 3.15am. The attack began at 5.00am when 10 Platoon caught a number of Japanese running down the hill to a bunker but at the same time were fired on from an enemy bunker further down the hill, and 11 Platoon alsocame under attack from all directions. Though they managed to take one bunker they also suffered a number of casualties. As a result Lowry ordered 12 Platoon to circle round to the right to attack the enemy's rear but they too encountered much enemy fire and got caught in a bunker. Then 11 and 12 Platoons reorganised themselves into one platoon and held their ground, which overlooked the enemy.

The battalion as a whole overran a few bunkers and held part of the hill, but the surrounding positions on GPT Ridge and DIS Hill were still in enemy hands. By the afternoon the north-west part of Jail Hill was captured and the men of Queen's Regiment had dug in, in mutually supporting positions. The battalion was reinforced by two platoons of

Gurkhas who helped take more Japanese defensive posts and brought up some more grenades, which had been running low. During the night it poured down and by the next day there were just two bunkers left. One was shelled by tanks which had finally got through to support the attack, having been held up by the poor weather and a Japanese road-block. The tanks fired only 15 yards in front of the forward troops. The soldiers of the Queen's Royal Regiment had to lie on their stomachs during the bombardment but there were no casualties and then the tanks used their 75mm automatics and a platoon occupied the bunker. The other bunker could not be reached by the tanks and was bombed with grenades by patrols and soon abandoned by the Japanese defenders. After the capture of Jail Hill it was found that the main bunker had steel shutters to deter grenades and could hold 50 Japanese soldiers. On 14 May the Queen's Royal Regiment was relieved by a Punjab battalion.

A memorial to all ranks of the 1st Battalion of the Queen's Royal Regiment who died in the battles for Jail Hill was made by the Battalion Pioneers and unveiled on 31 August 1944 by Lieutenant-General Stopford, GOC XXXIII Indian Corps. The memorial fell into disrepair and was finally replaced in 1972 by another in the Commonwealth War Graves Commission Cemetery at Kohima.

The centre of Kohima having now been cleared, on 22 May, 33rd Brigade took over the Naga village area. The Queen's Royal Regiment was in the south-east of the perimeter, the 4/15th Punjabis on their left and the 4/1st Gurkhas on the right. The Japanese positions were only about 100 yards away and the situation was said to resemble the trench warfare of the World War I. On 26 May the enemy attacked in strength but was repulsed by the brigade and fighting continued until 31 May, B Company eventually taking Church Knoll. On 1 June the battalion was withdrawn to Dimapur for rest and reinforcement. The enemy had put up a fanatical defence around Kohima and it took 2nd Division and 33rd Indian Brigade until June to clear the area of Japanese troops.

The brigade was back in action in the attack on Ukrul, an enemy communications centre. 33rd Brigade was to advance across country and attack from the north-west. The battalion was the rearguard, now down to fewer than 300 men. The going was very hard due to the heights, ridges and jungle growth that was encountered along the route. It took a whole day to cover eight miles. The first supply drop was on 1 July and on 6 July Ukrul was captured. The Queen's Royal Regiment undertook patrols until 26 July and then were moved back to Milestone 32 on the Kohima–Dimapur road where they remained for a month. On 6 September the Queen's Royal Regiment left the brigade as they were so under strength and went back to barracks in Shillong in Assam until March 1945 when they rejoined 7th Indian Division.

Going home

The trip home, in contrast to the three-month trip out to India, only took about two weeks as a result of the opening of the Suez Canal and now that the Mediterranean was clear of mines. The atmosphere on the way home was fairly relaxed, with sweepstakes taking place every day on how many miles the ship had travelled that day, and troops spending most of their time playing cards. Due to the cold, battle dress and greatcoats replaced the khaki drill and jungle greens.

An artist's impression of Jail Hill. (courtesy of the Trustees of the Imperial War Museum)

For some there were bands and a civic reception waiting at Liverpool and other docks when soldiers arrived back in the UK. Troops then hid their souvenirs as they passed through customs and boarded trains for the regimental depots, where soldiers received their pay, ration allowance and leave pass and were eventually allowed to go home for the first time, often after an absence of four years or more.

However, this was not always the case, as many returning soldiers from the Far East encountered indifference on their return, with no bands or welcoming committees, particularly after the end of the war in Europe. This only reinforced the image of the 'Forgotten Army' and soldiers often took a perverse pride in being forgotten on their return to 'Blighty' and

Trenches on DIS Hill looking towards the District Commissioner's bungalow. In the distance, to the right, is Kohima town and the Naga village beyond. (courtesy of the Trustees of the Imperial War Museum)

The road to Imphal soon after leaving Kohima. (courtesy of the Trustees of the Imperial War Museum)

Jeeps bringing supplies up through the mud on the Tiddim Trail. (courtesy of the Trustees of the Imperial War Museum)

ABOVE **The distances marched in the jungle could take a long time to cover. For example, one particular stretch of the Tiddim trail was called the 'chocolate staircase'. It climbed 3,000 feet in seven miles with many bends and a gradient of one in twelve and the slopes were continually being washed away in the monsoon so the soldiers had constantly to clear the track. The marches in Burma could go on for weeks with the same routine of march, stop, dig in, march, patrol, stand to, stand down, short rest, etc. The mules would carry the water and reserve ammunition in bulk panniers, with the soldiers carrying all their kit. The 'chocolate staircase' having been cleared of the enemy, a Dogra soldier armed with a Bren gun is protecting the river crossing at the foot of the hill. (courtesy of the Trustees of the Imperial War Museum)**

ABOVE **Dakotas dropping supplies to the 5th Indian Division on the Tiddim Road. (courtesy of the Trustees of the Imperial War Museum)**

took even greater pride in their bush hats and their 14th Army formation badges. On making his way home, Private Daniels recalled: 'My bush hat caused quite a bit of interest to the passengers on the bus and most eyes were on me as the bus arrived at Chartham bus stop and I alighted.'

Collecting

The nature of the climate and the distance from the UK combine to make it difficult for collectors to obtain material with good provenance relating to the war in the Far East. However, with patience, material can be found, albeit at a price.

Uniform and personal equipment such as webbing sets worn on operations will obviously be at a premium. The climate makes such items very susceptible to rot and rust and there was little incentive to bring such items back to the UK. However, unissued or post-war items made to the same design as wartime, particularly the 'jungle greens', may sometimes be found at militaria fairs, in dealers' catalogues or at auctions.

Weapons obviously pose a particular problem in the light of current security concerns and very stringent legal controls. There is a view that such items are not really suitable for the individual collector and anyone aspiring to such a collection would be advised to take expert advice. However, the law does not currently prevent people from owning real weapons that are fully deactivated under the current schedules to the firearms legislation. Such weapons are available from specialist dealers, again at a price, and it may well be possible to build up a representative selection of the types of rifles, pistols, light machine guns and even mortars that were used. Those looking for Japanese weapons, however, could well be in for a long and difficult search.

Perhaps the most promising area for the average collector is insignia. All British, African and Indian Army formations (armies, corps, divisions and some independent brigades) had a formation sign, a badge, usually cloth, that was worn by their constituent units on uniform sleeves, as slip-ons for epaulettes and sometimes on various forms of headdress. These badges were often colourful and with interesting designs (see colour plate G) and are still fairly readily available from militaria dealers. Many of the individual signs come in more than one variation as they were often provided by more than one manufacturer, or even made by hand. Much pleasure can be obtained from seeking out these badges and their many variations and the history of their development. Associated with formation signs are unit insignia, such as regimental cap badges and distinguishing flashes, again often in cloth, worn in association with the formation sign. Rank, along with trade, proficiency or prize insignia, is another branch of the same general area. Although, in the British Army at least, these are not theatre-specific they do often appear in materials

British troops admiring a Japanese good luck flag taken in action as a souvenir. (courtesy of the Trustees of the Imperial War Museum)

that were used overseas. For example, NCO's rank insignia can be found in khaki drill and in various metals for wearing on leather bands on the wrist where long-sleeved shirts or tunics would not be worn.

Printed material is also well worth considering. Two obvious areas are regimental and formation histories which tell in various degrees of detail the activities of, say, a division or a battalion, and campaign histories, including the official histories published by the British and Indian military establishments after the war, that tell the story of individual campaigns and battles. Biographies and autobiographies, along with individual memoirs, are good sources for a view from the trench or the turret, often providing highly idiosyncratic or tendentious accounts.

Officers of the 7th Indian Division at Pauk that the Division captured on 3 February 1945. (courtesy of the Trustees of the Imperial War Museum)

Another form of printed material is contemporary official publications. These come in various guises, from training pamphlets on quite narrow and specific subjects, such as an individual weapon, to guidance on broad subjects, such as tactics or supply and administration in the field. Other pamphlets can be classed as welfare or propaganda publications, dealing with things like war news and what today might be called civic studies. There are several such series of pamphlets that are specific to the Far Eastern theatre and they offer a fascinating glimpse of contemporary concerns and attitudes. Lastly Japanese occupation currency is widely available for purchase through militaria and antique fairs as it was produced in such large numbers.

Photographs are another area where the collector may find much of interest. The advances in photography between the wars had made cameras relatively cheap and available by World War II and one can often find individual photographs or even whole collections. Medals are another very collectible area ranging from the inexpensive unnamed campaign medal of the Burma star to medal groups and the rather more expensive named gallantry medals with associated provenance.

Other forms of souvenir were often brought back by individuals and have found their way onto the militaria market. Examples relevant to the Far Eastern theatre would include surrendered or found Japanese swords and flags, the most common of the latter being those covered with good luck messages from the soldier's family and friends. Some nurses collected formation insignia from their patients and friends and sewed them onto the inside of their capes, thus providing a very collectible, if now rare, item of interest to insignia collectors and others alike.

3in. mortar crews bombarding Meiktila with a Pagoda in the background. Meiktila was 80 miles south of Mandalay. (courtesy of the Trustees of the Imperial War Museum)

MUSEUMS

The following British museums have substantial collections relating to the British infantryman's experience of war in the Far East:

Imperial War Museum, Lambeth Road, London SE1 6HZ

There is an exhibition on the war in Burma entitled 'The Forgotten War' sponsored by the Burma Star Association, on display in the Land Warfare Hall at the Imperial War Museum's outstation at Duxford.

National Army Museum, Royal Hospital Road, Chelsea, London SW3 4HT

Kohima Museum, Imphal Barracks, Fulford Road, York YO10 4AU

The last-mentioned museum specifically relates to the 2nd Division's role at the battle of Kohima. The two following regimental museums are of interest at a battalion level:

The Queen's Royal Surrey Regiment Museum, Clandon House, West Clandon, Guildford, Surrey GU4 7RQ

Regimental Museum Argyll & Sutherland Highlanders, Stirling Castle, Stirling FK8 1EH

Details of other regimental museums can be found in Terry Wise's *A Guide to Military Museums and Other Places of Military Interest.*

The memorial to the soldiers of the Royal Welsh Fusiliers on Garrison Hill who gave their lives in the battles around Kohima. The monument bears the famous black flash of the regiment. This tradition of wearing the flash dates back to 1808, just before the Peninsular War, when queues or hair worn in tails was abolished and hair was cut short again. The Royal Welsh Fusiliers were based in Nova Scotia at this period and continued to wear queues; even when the regiment ceased to wear queues the officers continued to wear the queue ribbon. This was noticed by the inspecting general officer who ordered its removal. However, the colonel of the regiment obtained the king's consent for the regiment's officers to continue wearing the flash and it was extended to all ranks in 1900. Another regimental tradition was observed by the Royal Welsh Fusiliers while in action during the First Arakan campaign. 'Eating the leek' was when the last-joined recruit of the regiment ate a leek on St David's Day. In Burma, as there were no leeks available, a shallot was eaten with curry powder and egg white. (courtesy of the Trustees of the Imperial War Museum)

BIBLIOGRAPHY

Primary sources held in the Department of Printed Books and the Department of Documents

Daniels Mss. Papers of Private C. E. Daniels, 95/33/1

Gumbrell Mss. Papers of Private R. R. Gumbrell, 99/46/1

Major G. R. Storry, *Service with the Intelligence Corps in India and Burma March 1942 to May 1943* (TS Memoir, 1946–1947), 01/34/2

Brigadier F. H. Vinden, *By Chance a Soldier* (unpublished Mss.), 96/36/1

GHQ India, MTP No. 9 (India), *Notes on Forest Warfare* (India, Simla, 1940)

GHQ India, MTP No. 9 (India), *The Jungle Book* (4th edition, India, September 1943)

Malaya Command, *Tactical Notes for Malaya* (Malaya, 1940)

Brigadier M. C. Morgan, *Army Welfare* (War Office, 1953)

Lieutenant-Colonel J. H. A. Sparrow, *Morale* (War Office, 1949)

The War Office, *Notes from Theatres of War No. 19: Burma, 1943/44* (1945)

The War Office, MTP No. 52, *Warfare in the Far East* (December 1944)

Secondary sources

Louis Allen, *Burma: The Longest War 1941–1945* (London: Dent, 1984)

Louis Allen, *Singapore, 1941–1942* (London: Davis-Poynter, 1972)

John Colvin, *Not Ordinary Men: The Battle of Kohima re-assessed* (London: Leo Cooper, 1994)

J. P. Cross, *Jungle Warfare: Experiences and Encounters* (London: Guild Publishing, 1989)

Major R. C. G. Foster, *History of the Queen's Royal Regiment Vol. VIII 1924–1948* (Aldershot: Gale & Polden, 1953)

David Fraser, *And We Will Shock Them. The British Army in the Second World War* (London: Hodder and Stoughton, 1983)

George Macdonald Fraser, *Quartered Safe Out Here* (London: Harvill, 1992)

Roy Humphreys, *To Stop a Rising Sun: Reminiscences of Wartime in India and Burma* (Stroud, Gloucestershire: Alan Sutton Publishing Ltd., 1996)

Major-General S. Woodburn Kirby, *History of the Second World War: The War against Japan* Vols. 1–5 (London: HMSO, 1957-1959)

Major M. A. Lowry, *An Infantry Company in Arakan and Kohima* (Aldershot: Gale & Polden, 1950)

Brigadier M. R. Roberts, *Golden Arrow: The Story of the 7th Indian Division in the Second World War 1939–1945* (Aldershot: Gale & Polden, 1952)

John Shipster, *Mist over the Rice Fields* (Barnsley: Leo Cooper, 2000)

Field-Marshal Sir William Slim, *Defeat into Victory* (London: Cassell, 1952)

David Smurthwaite (editor), *The Forgotten War: British Army in the Far East 1941–1945* (London: National Army Museum, 1992)

Brigadier I. M. Stewart, *The Thin Red Line: 2nd Argylls in Malaya* (London: Nelson, 1947)

COLOUR PLATE COMMENTARY

A: SOLDIER, 2ND BATTALION, ARGYLL AND SUTHERLAND HIGHLANDERS

This soldier is wearing a tropical pith helmet, KD shirt and shorts (the shorts nicknamed 'Bombay bloomers'), gaiters and boots. His equipment includes the 1937-pattern webbing.

1. A *dhah*, Indian-made knife.
2. Sealed pattern of a KD jacket of a warrant officer class 1, Scottish or Highland regiment. This one has the brass shoulder titles, A&SH, of the Argyll and Sutherland Highlanders.
3. KD bush shirt.

B: TRAINING

The training of the 2nd Battalion, Argyll and Sutherland Highlanders, attracted publicity. In particular, the march back to Singapore from Mersing, a distance of 61 miles that was achieved in three days, was widely reported in the *Straits Times* and even in Britain..

By the end of the two month training periood, the trainees were expected to march 40km (25 miles) per day with full equipment.

Troops were taught how to take advantage of the natural resources of the jungle. Fish, vegetables and fruit were utilised in order to pad out the staple diet of rice, tea, sugar and salt. Note the men wear khaki drill uniform that was replaced by the jungle-green type in 1943.

C: JUNGLE TRAINING

Three British troops training in the Indian jungle during 1944 before being posted to Burma. They are wearing camouflaged tin helmets in order to blend into the jungle, and are armed with No. 4 rifles and a Bren gun. They are keeping silent in order to surprise the enemy in an ambush.

The British attitude towards the jungle changed during the 1930s after a series of surveys and exercises that were carried out.

Previously the jungle had been considered impenetrable for troops but by 1940 there were two training manuals instructing troops on manoeuvring and fighting in this hazadous terrain, However, due to a lack of central directive from Malaya Command, most units i instead relied upon experienced personnel as a basis for training until the *Jungle Book* was introduced in September 1943. This included photographs and cartoons to make it appeal to the men.

Note the men wear the jungle-green uniform that replaced the khaki drill.

Lord Louis Mountbatten reading the order of the day from the steps of the municipal building in Singapore after the surrender had been signed by the Japanese. (courtesy of the Trustees of the Imperial War Museum)

D: TACTICS

An example of tactics for defence and attack in the jungle:

1. The enemy is encountered while advancing along a track. To prevent their flanking movement, troops would be sent out to counter the envelopment. This was an example of aggressive defence.

2. In attack, the recce patrols would be sent forward to determine the strength and position of the enemy. Then a feint of a small number of fighting patrols would attack on one flank, while the main body of troops would attack on the opposite flank and from the rear.

E: AMBUSH

Two types of ambush used in the jungle:

1. The quickest method of ambush was to form a road-block against the advancing enemy troops. Troops would attack the enemy from concealed positions in the jungle from either side of the track and also bring machine guns into action at the rear of the enemy.

2. Ambushing the enemy on a track when their movement of direction was unknown was more difficult. Ambush parties would be positioned on the track in both directions in order to oppose the enemy coming from either direction. The position that did not come into contact with the enemy would then outflank the enemy and assist the other position. Mortar parties would be placed on the road to attack the halted enemy and, after the ambush parties had withdrawn, they could fire on the confused enemy troops while being protected by a covering party.

A well-camouflaged soldier in training, armed with a Bren gun Mark 1. (courtesy of the Trustees of the Imperial War Museum)

F: WEAPONS

Weapons used by British troops in the Far East:
1. Rifle No. 4 Mark 1.
2. Rifle No. 5 with bayonet.
3. Bren gun Mark 1.
4. M1928 Thompson submachine gun.
5. No. 36 hand grenade or mills bomb.
6. Sten gun Mark 2.
7. Enfield .38 Mark 1 pistol.
8. PIAT (Projector, infantry, anti-tank).
9. Boys anti-tank rifle.

G: BADGES AND FORMATION SIGNS

1. Cap badge of the Argyll and Sutherland Highland Regiment (Princess Louise's).

2. Cap badge of the Queen's Royal Regiment (West Surrey). It is thought that the Paschal lamb derives from one of its predecessor regiments, the Tangier Regiment, who fought the Moors in Morroco in the seventeenth century. The regiment merged with the East Surrey Regiment in 1958 to form the Queen's Royal Surrey Regiment.

The following formation signs cover all the divisions in which British infantrymen served in the Far East.

3. 2nd British Infantry Divisional formation sign. The badge was chosen in 1940 by the then GOC, Major-General H. Charles Lloyd. It is said to derive from the arms of the Archbishop of York and to be a reference to the time when Britain used to raise two armies, the second being from the north. 2nd Division was a regular division at the outbreak of World War II and it formed part of the British Expeditionary Force in France and Belgium in 1940. It was transferred to India in June 1942 and went into action in Burma as part of 14th Army in March 1944.

4. 36th British Division. The division was raised in early 1943 as an Indian Army formation, consisting of the 29th British Brigade and 72nd Indian Brigade. The Divisional badge was an amalgamation of the two individual brigade signs, the white circle for the 29th and the red for the 72nd. On 1 September 1944, the division was redesignated as British and on 14th December it received the 26th Indian Brigade as its third brigade. It took part in operations in the Arakan before moving to Ledo when it came under the command of General Stillwell's Chinese–American Army under which it fought around Myitkyina and Mogaung. In January 1945 the division crossed the Irrawaddy and advanced into the Shan States, coming under 14th Army command. It returned to India in June 1945 and was disbanded along with 26th Brigade in September.

5. 3rd Indian Division (Chindits) formed in August 1943. This was not strictly speaking a division at all but a cover name for a special long-range penetration and raiding force. It was made up from elements of other formations, including 70th Division, and operated as a number of columns of approximately battalion size. The main element of the sign is the *chinthe*, the golden Burmese dragon that guards Buddhist temples. In the background is a representation of a pagoda. The name 'Chindit' arose from a mishearing by General Orde Wingate, the formation's original commander, of the word *chinthe*, but the error remained uncorrected and the name stuck.

6. 5th Indian Division was formed in June 1940 and the formation sign was nicknamed the 'ball of fire', (as well as other, less polite, soldiers' sobriquets) and it derived from red circles that were hurriedly painted on the division's vehicles when it was ordered that divisional signs were ordered to be displayed. The formation served in the Middle East, Western Desert and in Burma.

7. 7th Indian Division, known as the 'Golden Arrow' Division. The division was formed in Attock on the north-west frontier on 1 October 1941, which region it was raised to protect. The badge symbolised the direction of line of advance on the north-west frontier. The division served on the north-east frontier and in Burma. There are examples of the gold arrows in metal worn on a square black cloth backing being worn as a formation sign. Very similar golden arrow brooches were given to each member of the local Women's Volunteer Service when the division left Chhindwara at the end of training.

8. 9th Indian Division was formed in Malaya in September 1940 and was defeated and went into captivity in Malaya in February 1942.

9. 11th Indian Division was formed in Malaya in October 1940. The badge was still in use at Changi prisoner-of-war camp in Singapore where it adorned the entrance. The division included the British Battalion which was an amalgamation of the 1st Leicesters and the 2nd East Surrey Regiments formed after the heavy losses sustained in the retreat from northern Malaya.

10. 14th Indian Division was raised at Quetta in May 1942 by Major-General H. H. Rich. The central peak of the mountain range represents Mount Takatu, 10,000 feet high, overlooking Quetta, which is itself represented by the Q-shaped border of the badge. The division served in Assam on the Burma–India border and in the first Arakan after which it was redesignated as a training division, in June 1942.

11. 17th Indian Division was raised in Ahmednagar in 1941 under the command of Major-General Sir John Smyth VC. The original sign had been a streak of lightning but after the Japanese radio propagandist, Tokyo Rose, had called it the division whose sign was a yellow streak and it had been driven out of Burma, the lucky black cat was adopted. Two of the original brigades served in Malaya and one in the retreat from Burma. It was present at both the loss and the retaking of Rangoon under its commander Major General 'Punch' Cowan.

12. 19th Indian Division, otherwise known as the 'Dagger' Division. It was originally formed in India in 1941 under Major-General Sir John Smyth VC before he took over 17th Indian Division. The sign was designed and drawn by his wife, Frances. It was later commanded by the inspirational Major-General T. Wynford (Pete) Rees and was instrumental in the capture of Mandalay, where they raised the Union Jack over Fort Dufferin on 20 March 1945.

13. 20th Indian Division was raised in Bangalore in 1942 under Major-General Douglas Gracey. The division was trained solely for jungle warfare in Ceylon before seeing action in Assam and Burma, where it fought in the Imphal plain and the Irrawaddy. The sign was selected to symbolise the 'swift and deadly execution' of the Japanese Army.

14. 23rd Indian Division was formed at Ranchi in January 1942. The sign was designed by Major-General Savory, who later went on to play a vital role as Director of Infantry Training. The red fighting cock was intended to be symbolic to both British and Indian Army troops while not alienating

Hindu or Muslim troops It was also intended to be capable of a slightly bawdy interpretation. General Savory said that frequently he had to insist that the result was 'a fighting cock, not a bloody rooster'.

15. 25th Indian Division was set up in Southern India under Major-General H. L. (Taffy) Davies and was nicknamed the 'Ace of Spades' Division. The division fought in the third Arakan campaign.

16. 26th Indian Division was raised in April 1942 and was nicknamed the 'Tiger Head' Division after the Royal Bengal tiger stepping out of a triangle. The triangle was a pun on the Greek letter Delta as the Division was formed on the Hoogli delta from the HQ Presidency and the Assam District. The division fought in the second and third Arakan campaigns and in the recapture of Rangoon.

17. 39th Indian Division was originally formed as 1st Burma Division – 'Burdiv' – in July 1941 until 1942 and then was redesignated the 38th Light Indian Division. As there was a Chinese 38th Division in theatre after just one day it became the 39th Light Indian Division. It became a training division in 1943.

18. 81st West African Division was formed on 1 March 1943 in Nigeria. It was the first division ever to be formed from the units of the West African Frontier Force drawn from each of the four West African colonies of Nigeria, the Gold Coast, Sierra Leone and Gambia. The division went to India in August 1943. Its commander, General Woolner, chose the sign, which represented Ananse, a figure in Ashanti mythology who could overcome his enemies through guile. The badge was worn head down so it would appear going forward when a soldier was about to fire his weapon. The press thought it was tarantula but these were not indigenous to West Africa and not black.

19. 82nd West African Division was formed in Nigeria in August 1943 and dispatched to India in July 1944. The badge depicted two spears crossed on a native carrier's headband and symbolised 'Through our carriers we fight', showing the important part the carriers played in the movement and supply of the division.

20. 11th East African Division was raised in central area, east Africa, and sent to Ceylon in June 1943. The first pattern of the badge was a brown rhino's head on a buff oval background, which was later changed to a black head on a red oval.

H: SOLDIER, 1ST BATTALION, QUEEN'S ROYAL REGIMENT

This soldier is wearing a bush hat, jungle-green battle dress, 1937 webbing, a bandoleer containing ammunition and holding a Rifle No. 4.

1. *Kukri*, a Gurkha knife, very popular with British troops in the jungle.

2. 24-hour supper ration pack with some of its contents: a packet of oatmeal, tin of ham and egg, a packet of anti-malarial mepracrine tablets and a packet of Craven cigarettes. The American packs offered three meals, a pack for breakfast, lunch and supper, with a value of 4,200 calories. The normal calorie intake for the British public was 2,900. The packs included mepacrine, two packets of cigarettes, canned ham and eggs, chocolate and salt tablets to counter the effects of perspiration.

3. K ration dinner pack. K rations were developed by Dr Ancel Keys of the University of Minnesota and contained a well-balanced meal that was ready to eat. They consisted of a tin of meat, such as Spam, and one of cheese spread, two wooden spoons, a pack of toilet paper, chewing gum, packets of cigarettes, instant coffee, soap cubes, sugar, biscuits and chocolate.

4. A colonel's jungle-green bush jacket .

5. Olive-green cellular bush shirt introduced in 1944.

6. Basic webbing pouch, 1937 pattern, which has been blancoed dark green in order to fit in with the new jungle greens.

Welsh soldiers who were released after the Japanese surrender in Singapore. They had endured three and half years of extreme privation and hardship as prisoners of war. (courtesy of the Trustees of the Imperial War Museum)

INDEX

Figures in **bold** refer to illustrations.

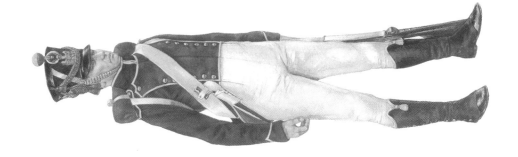

FIND OUT MORE ABOUT OSPREY

❑ Please send me the latest listing of Osprey's publications

❑ I would like to subscribe to Osprey's e-mail newsletter

Title/rank

Name

Address

Postcode/zip   state/country

e-mail

I am interested in:

❑ Ancient world
❑ Medieval world
❑ 16th century
❑ 17th century
❑ 18th century
❑ Napoleonic
❑ 19th century

❑ American Civil War
❑ World War I
❑ World War II
❑ Modern warfare
❑ Military aviation
❑ Naval warfare

Please send to:

USA & Canada:
Osprey Direct USA, c/o MBI Publishing, P.O. Box 1, 729 Prospect Avenue, Osceola, WI 54020

UK, Europe and rest of world:
Osprey Direct UK, P.O. Box 140, Wellingborough, Northants, NN8 2FA, United Kingdom

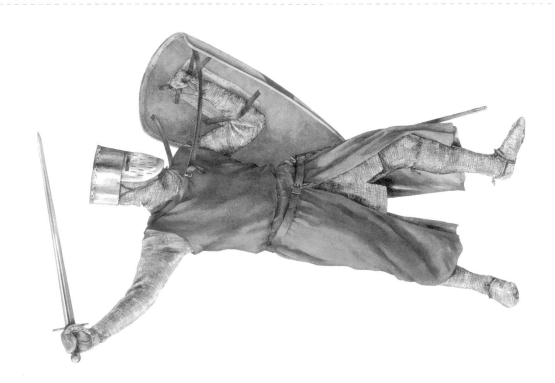

OSPREY
PUBLISHING

www.ospreypublishing.com

call our telephone hotline
for a free information pack

USA & Canada: 1-800-826-6600
UK, Europe and rest of world call:
+44 (0) 1933 443 863

Young Guardsman
Figure taken from *Warrior 22:*
Imperial Guardsman 1799–1815
Published by Osprey
Illustrated by Christa Hook

Knight, c.1190
Figure taken from *Warrior 1: Norman Knight 950 – 1204 AD*
Published by Osprey
Illustrated by Christa Hook

POSTCARD